UNDERNEATH MY CLOTHES

A woman's guide to making peace with her body

Jo Ettles

JoJo
PUBLISHING

Underneath My Clothes
Jo Ettles

Published by Classic Author and Publishing Services Pty Ltd.
Imprint of JoJo Publishing.
First published 2015

Copyright © 2015 Jo Ettles
ISBN: 9780987144829

JoJo Publishing

Editor: Merryl Scott
Designer / typesetter: Working Type Studio (www.workingtype.com.au)
Printed in Australia by Lightning Source

National Library of Australia Cataloguing-in-Publication entry

Creator:	Ettles, Jo, author.
Title:	Underneath my clothes / Jo Ettles (author); Merryl Scott (editor).
ISBN:	9780987144829 (paperback)
Subjects:	Self-acceptance.
	Self-actualization (Psychology)
	Conduct of life.
	Other Creators/Contributors:
	Scott, Merryl, editor.
Dewey Number:	158.1

When and who decided that we should be judged solely by size and appearance? Why do so many of us set our mood for the day according to what number we hit when we stand on the bathroom scales? Why do so many equate weight loss and being thin to being successful and beautiful? I dedicate *Underneath my Clothes* to every person who is challenged by their personal insecurities. Whether it is weight issues or low self-esteem, if you consistently struggle to acknowledge your own beauty, I wrote this book for you. When we cease the fight and quit the negative internal dialogue; when we embrace our body and accept our uniqueness, no matter what form it takes; when we acknowledge our own self-worth; when we take full responsibility for our health; when we treat our body with the respect that it deserves; when we nurture, nourish, move and whole heartedly accept ourselves, it is only then that we can release our spirit from struggle, find peace and start to feel light.

In loving memory of my beautiful nana
Matilda Caroline Waterman, 1910–2003

Contents

Introduction

Self-esteem has never been a problem for me. I have always struggled however with my body in some way. Allergies, weight gain, weight loss, over-eating, under-eating, yoyo dieting, you name it; I have experienced it. What accompanies all these highs and lows are all sorts of emotions. Finally, after more than fifty years on the planet, I have learnt to manage and understand my delicate constitution and accept and respect myself, curves and all. For the last eight years, I have had the absolute privilege of working as a wellness consultant. Sharing so many people's battles with food, weight, body issues and self-esteem has taught me why it is important to stop the internal fight that we often have with ourselves. I have learnt that it is vital for each and every one of us to deeply love and respect our body, mind and spirit. It is absolutely paramount for us to acknowledge all of the beautiful qualities that we have been blessed with. Self-love and self-acceptance are the foundation of wellness.

I remember consulting with two sisters some years ago. They had pretty much done and dusted the whole diet circuit: Pre-packaged diet meals, shakes, high protein foods only, soup diets; you name it, they had tried it. None of these options had offered a permanent solution to their ongoing food battles. They were ready to quit dieting and embrace healthy eating as a lifestyle. One sister wanted to lose about twenty kilos, the other sister wanted to lose about five kilos. I remember thinking at the consultation, "Five kilos! That's a piece of cake," pardon the pun. What I learnt from these two sisters at that initial consultation was that no matter what the challenge, whether it is body image or low self-esteem, whether it is five kilos or fifty kilos, the emotions associated with the issue feel pretty much the same for everyone. It can feel overwhelmingly heavy, frustrating and all consuming.

Sadly, most people arrived at my office at their absolute lowest ebb. Not knowing how to take those vital steps forward that would bring change and freedom were challenging. I was constantly overwhelmed at how a client's body language and energy reflected every emotion that they were feeling at that initial first meeting. Physically and verbally they expressed frustration, while they remained completely focussed on everything that was weighing them down. Each client made sure I heard every single thing that they despised about themselves. Although my job was to educate clients on eating healthy food as a lifestyle, I soon found out that the key to unlocking the struggle was to change the way people viewed themselves as a whole. When people look at themselves through the eyes of love, they are quickly released from their internal struggles. Combining self-love, acceptance and appreciation for all your body does, with an education on healthy nurturing food, is a recipe for success.

For many who arrived at my office, I am positive that they thought I had a magic wand placed in my drawer and once I had heard their issues, I would just wave the wand and sprinkle them with my magic 'I want to be skinny' dust and Violà! Issues begone! They would skip out of my office and feel like a brand new person. Well, unfortunately for them, I didn't have a magic wand and I didn't have magic skinny dust. I did however have the ability to shower each and every client with uplifting energy and hope. Hope that if they changed their focus as well as their diet, they could completely achieve wellness on every level and then they would really feel like a brand new person.

The secret to feeling beautiful, in my opinion, is quite simply this, manage your challenges, take responsibility for every aspect of your life and speak to yourself as you would someone you loved. Negativity has to be one of the most destructive energies of all. Make the decision daily to look at yourself and your world and see the abundant beauty. I choose to see every part of my make-up as something special and beautiful. I fully embrace and accept myself and I am committed to appreciating all that is me every single day. Beauty must be seen in your own eyes first.

You can literally change your life right now. Let your self-image be a reflection of the true you and dig down as deep as you can and acknowledge all the amazing qualities that you have inside and out. Let them shine through. Make the commitment to nurture your body, your mind and your spirit with elements that will ensure you are illuminated in every way. In this book, I share my highs and lows with you, my vulnerabilities, my struggles and my journey to making peace with my body. I hope that through my experiences, you discover just how incredible you are. If you think you are the only one in the world facing challenges, think again! You are not alone. Often the person you least expect is struggling with some issue. The secret to self-acceptance is how you view your challenges and how you manage them.

Every chapter of your life, just like this book, is a part of your story. If you are experiencing low self-esteem, body image issues or have developed negative, bad habits, I encourage you to turn the page. You have the opportunity to begin a new chapter. Today is a perfect day to change your life and make peace with your body.

"Challenges are what make life interesting and overcoming them is what makes life meaningful."
—Joshua J. Marine

PART ONE

I Am Woman

5

Chapter One

Ginger Meggs

I was born in 1963. As far as I know, I was a fairly healthy baby. I honestly can't remember my life before the age of about four or five years. I do remember little things that happened and have occasional flashbacks, but everything is vividly clear from school age. The memories that are the strongest in my childhood are those that are associated with sickness, nothing serious, but certainly niggling afflictions which were severe enough to affect normal day-to-day life. Often the symptoms of these afflictions were amplified because I just didn't know how to handle the discomfort associated with them. Pale skinned and covered with freckles, I was nicknamed Ginger Meggs by Mum and Dad; Ginger Meggs was a mischievous, freckled-faced male cartoon character made famous in the 1920s. That should help you visualise my appearance. I don't think I was that mischievous, but I guess the pale skin and freckles topped off with strawberry blonde hair conjured up some similarities. I am still a little confused as to why they nicknamed me after a boy but, I shouldn't be offended as Mum and Dad nicknamed my older sister 'Goog'. Isn't that an

Australian slang term for a hardboiled egg? I guess it was the 60s so I will cut them some slack.

Mum has always been a really warm, loving cook especially when my entire family were all living at home. She took great pride in preparing filling homely meals for us daily. You would always find a fresh loaf of warm white bread on the counter after school. She would often make a shepherd's pie for dinner, laden with soft creamy potatoes all golden and brown, and her signature dish was lemon meringue pie. Soft delicate crust filled with the smoothest of lemon filling and meringue that seemed to peak about half a metre high. She would bake biscuits and cakes and lovely meals all the time and our house often smelt of garlic and onions freshly sautéed. The garlic and onion fried was a trick she often pulled at about 6pm just before Dad got home from work. It tricked us all into thinking that a gourmet meal was being prepared. I have since learnt it was a sign that she had absolutely no idea what she was going to feed us and this little fry-up would allow her some time to think of something practical, affordable and easy to put on the table.

So what did we eat in the 1960s? Well, we didn't eat pre-packaged meals or fatty, take-away dinners that's for sure; it was mainly meat and three vegetables. Eggs, wheat flour, white sugar and butter were all used for cooking staples. Cakes and slices were made from eggs, butter, flour and a little icing sugar. A normal day for me as a child would include, toast with Vegemite for breakfast. At school, it was traditional that at 10am, we would all have to drink a bottle of full cream milk. This milk was usually warm, as it would have been delivered earlier in the day and left outside the classroom in the sun until recess. Lunch would be a sandwich and an apple. After school, well I would eat tons of that beautiful fresh white bread and dinner would be meat and vegetables; think roast meat, mash potatoes and peas. This type of menu was commonly served in most middle class households in Australia.

I definitely didn't have any weight issues as a child; I was quite lanky and thin. I would walk to school, run around and play outside until 5pm every night. I was really active and busy, every weekend playing netball. I was fit and lean, but I was plagued with ailments, nothing serious or sinister, but just constant irritations and allergies causing endless frustration. I suffered with sinusitis, headaches, hives, eczema, skin rashes, itching and I think Mum was convinced that I was a bit of a hypochondriac to be honest. It wasn't until I was well into my thirties, that all those symptoms I had suffered as a child were diagnosed as being associated with food allergies. Growing up, my diet consisted of far too much wheat and sugar. It was just too much for my system to handle.

I also suffered with chronic eczema as a child and it itched so badly it would often bleed. My sinuses were continuously blocked and it felt like I had a permanent headache. The full cream milk that was compulsory to drink at school would aggravate my sinuses and make the symptoms a hundred times worse. In spring when the flowers were beginning to blossom, my allergies would escalate even more. I often had stomach aches and generally felt lousy. Nowadays, a child presenting with similar issues would be encouraged to eliminate wheat, sugar, dairy and gluten to see if their health improved. We have loads of alternatives available now to use as replacements, so it is far easier to manage food allergies and intolerances in today's society. Back then, had you eliminated all those foods, there would have been little to eat for those of us raised in mainstream suburban households.

It was pretty common though that most people were consuming lots of white flour, lots of white sugar and dairy. Obesity wasn't really a big problem. It probably was to a degree, but we didn't have the same mediums constantly broadcasting what was happening in the world as intensely as we do today. Serving sizes were smaller; nothing was supersized. In the 1960s, a normal dinner plate was around twenty-three centimetres in diameter compared to today's dinner plate which is approximately thirty-one centimetres, so we can fit a whole lot more food on our plates. There were very few takeouts except fresh fish and hot chips wrapped in newspaper which was the only take away option available. Life was very different back then. There were no computers or video games and Disneyland on Sunday afternoons was the only TV show that I was allowed to watch.

Looking back, the main issue with my niggling health issues was purely from what I was eating. My sensitive system just couldn't tolerate certain foods. I am unsure why the doctors back then didn't really recognise the fact that my system was reacting to many different elements. For well over two thousand years there has been plenty of medical recognition that food can cause illnesses, disease and major health concerns for certain individuals. It took me until I was an adult to self-diagnose that I was suffering food allergies and food intolerances. The expressions 'food allergy' as well as 'food intolerance' are generally used to describe an unpleasant reaction to food, resulting in some awful irritating symptoms. Eczema and asthma are often associated with food allergies. Migraines, vomiting and diarrhoea are often associated with food intolerances. I had both, so I had no idea what was an allergy and what was an intolerance because there were so many different symptoms.

Eczema is an awfully painful condition and I remember my episodes clearly. An itchy, red, angry rash appears often on the face, on the skin behind the knees and elbows and in severe cases, all over the body. The skin becomes cracked often bleeding and weeping and it itches like crazy. It is so unpleasant and emotionally distressing; you can't think straight or even sleep properly from the terrible itching and pain associated with it. Mine was mainly on my legs and arms and although really painful, I have seen far worse cases of eczema than what I experienced on children in clinics I have been in. Research shows there are countless triggers for eczema such as cows' milk, eggs, fish, nuts; almost any food can trigger an episode. Research also shows that even house dust mites and pet fur can trigger an attack. It is different for everyone so it can be quite challenging to manage.

These outbreaks of eczema, hives, sinusitis and stomach aches seemed to go on well into my teenage years and if that wasn't enough, with the onset of puberty my face broke out in the worst case of acne. Now you would think with all those visual afflictions that I would have retreated to my bedroom waiting the day when I would wake up having been transformed into a beautiful swan, but retreating wasn't really my style. I do remember crying desperately from the discomfort and despair at times, but that was mainly a response to the symptoms I was experiencing. Once the pain eased or subsided, I was very quick to pull myself together and get back into enjoying life. Although now, when I look back, I never wanted to be too far away from Mum as she was the one who would cover me with calamine lotion, bathe me in warm water to soothe the itching and reassure me that it would eventually pass.

It really became the norm to be suffering from some allergy on a daily basis. During puberty, the eczema subsided thank goodness; I guess the universe decided acne and eczema were just too much for one teenage girl to cope with. The sinusitis continued and I could handle that with preventative sprays. When I was about sixteen, the acne quite simply vanished. All of a sudden, the many dreadful ailments as if by magic disappeared. It was like my fairy godmother had flown into my room one night and waved her magic wand over me and blessed me with a reprieve. She had cut me some slack and released me from feeling trapped inside my aggravated system. Everyone should have a fairy godmother like that!

Despite the niggling challenges though, my self-esteem was still firmly intact. I was so grateful to not be uncomfortable in my own skin anymore. I remember looking in the mirror and being completely overwhelmed by my clear complexion, not just on my face, but on my whole body. To not be in pain, to not be physically marked with obvious irritation, to feel whole so to speak was such an incredible feeling. To this day, I remember that sense of freedom and wellness I felt when things subsided. Although a little apprehensive that it was a temporary reprieve from my fairy godmother, day by day I realised that perhaps I had grown out of some of these debilitating afflictions and I was now able to feel normal – well as normal as I would ever be. It felt amazing.

I look back at those years and I realise that my childhood allergies have made me today extremely tolerant, strong and a trifle unsympathetic to those who have a low pain threshold. The experience taught me that, no matter how fractured or damaged the exterior is, what is inside is the true measure of someone's strength and beauty. As kids, a lot of our foundations for the future are firmly cemented. When I was hurting, Mum would constantly repeat to me, "You're ok, you're ok. Come on now, get up, you will be fine". The inside of me was inflamed and the outside was irritated, but Mum was right, my spirit was firmly intact and her continual reassurance allowed me to push forward.

We can't turn back the clock and change the past, but we can certainly look back and learn from every experience. Each and every one of us has the power to take a negative and turn it into a positive. Through my food allergies and intolerances, I have been able to assist people suffering with similar issues. Encouraging people in similar situations to start with examining their diet as a step forward towards managing allergies and body issues is my way of acknowledging why I had to experience those afflictions as a child. You have the power to take any situation, any experience and literally turn it into a positive experience. Although challenging to do when you are in the midst of pain and angst, you will be amazed at how much strength and determination you actually possess when you believe that, 'You are ok, you are actually ok'. What have you experienced or what are you experiencing that may be overwhelming? Look at whatever it is head on and really examine the root cause of the issue.

Once you identify the underlying problems, no matter what they are, take the vital steps to eliminate them from your life. Day by day, as you heal and regain your strength, challenge yourself to look back briefly and turn your experience into an opportunity to show the world your resilience. Can something take your confidence, your strength, your determination away? Only if you let it!

"The food you eat can either be the safest and most powerful form of medicine or the slowest form of poison."
—Ann Wigmore

Chapter Two

Does my bum look big in this?

I wasn't particularly athletic growing up; I played netball but that was the extent of my sporting career. I had tried swimming and nearly drowned in a shallow pool; I had tried gymnastics and fell head first off the bar. Mum put me into deportment and modelling classes when I was about ten years old as modelling classes seemed like the safest option. I remember my first day at Joyce Smith's modelling academy in Perth. Mum drove me into the city to the studio all dressed up in my very best outfit. To this day, I can still feel the emotions associated with that very first visit. I walked up the stairs to the classroom where professional photos of beautiful models, male and female, adorned the walls. This elegant, young woman was at reception and welcomed us to the school. Mum was advised to wait downstairs until the lesson was over so I went and sat down with twelve other girls in the class. I just remember thinking how pretty everyone was. I was still very much in my 'Ginger Meggs' phase, so I was fairly awkward, but my self-confidence was pretty unshakeable. I wasn't nervous at all to join the class; it felt so right for me to be there and that I belonged.

When I look back now at photos of myself at that age, I have often asked my mum, "Why, why, oh why did you cut my hair like Moe from the Three Stooges?" I am quite positive that this particular haircut was not in fashion, unless of course you were auditioning for a role in the Three Stooges. I will do my best to create an accurate visual for you of this hairstyle just in case you weren't around in the 1970s. Ok, the hair is strawberry blonde in colour, the stylist, disguised as my mother, places a plastic mixing bowl over my head. Huge dressmaking scissors are removed from Singer sewing machine table and creatively cut the hair hanging from underneath the bowl to mirror the shape of the rim of the bowl. The bowl is removed, new hairstyle is revealed and the end result … drumroll please (make sound of drum roll here, thankyou) … HORRENDOUS!

Mum's way of explaining this unique style was, "Well, you wouldn't let me curl your hair, you wouldn't sit still long enough for me to plait it and when I did curl it, you would rip all the bobby pins out. Cutting it this way was practical and tidy." I have said to Mum over the years, "I looked like a boy" and she still to this day is always very quick to respond with, "Oh no, absolutely not. You were beautiful." It's obvious to me now that Mum's reassuring words describing what she could see through her eyes as my mother, was the foundation for my very strong self-esteem. You see, I believed everything my mum said to me. Why wouldn't I?

If you are a parent, it's really important to understand that positive communication is essential to building your child's self-esteem. Children and adults thrive on words that convey reassurance, encouragement, love and praise and actually stopping and really listening to your children is a vital part of creating strong self-esteem.

I loved modelling; it was so much fun. I never felt nervous when stepping onto a catwalk and I felt extremely comfortable. Those lessons were really empowering. We were encouraged to shine. I remember sitting in front of a mirror in the classroom where the teacher would ask us to acknowledge everything we liked about ourselves. When we finished this exercise, we were then asked to face our classmates and express what we liked about them. Talk about topping up our self-esteem tanks! That teacher drilled into us how fantastic we all were; it was two hours weekly of self-love boot camp.

I continued modelling for years. When I was fifteen, I was appointed assistant to the modelling teacher. In this role I would welcome students into the class, demonstrate how to walk the runway, the turns, posture and assist anyone who was feeling self-conscious. I felt so important and I had definitely shaken the old Ginger Meggs image off by then. I was tall for my age; my hair was now long, wavy and streaked from the sun and I seemed to tower over girls my own age in height. At sixteen years of age I took a part-time job with a fashion company and it was at this point that my weight started to fluctuate. I was modelling part-time and I moved swiftly up the ranks with the fashion house to become a full-time manager of one of their biggest stores.

Eating healthily wasn't a priority at this stage; I was young and my metabolism was fast and furious. I managed a team of fabulous, fun girls in this boutique and we would work such long hours together. I was directing a huge team of fashion stylists, attending fashion production meetings, working on fashion parades, as well as keeping the store positioned as the best performing store in the country. It was really fast paced and my role was demanding. The fashion store was located in a huge shopping centre in Perth and the food court seemed to be overflowing with unhealthy food. I am sure if I could take a trip back in time to those days, I would see that there were probably some really healthy food choices available to us but I seemed to be drawn to the unhealthy foods naturally, so perhaps I just didn't notice them. Lunch time with the girls seemed to be a celebration of all things bad for us. We all did a fabulous job of encouraging each other to choose the unhealthiest lunches available in the centre. Chinese food or toasted sandwiches covered in butter, laden with ham and melted cheese, nothing was off limits. Later in the afternoon, one of the girls would nip out for some chocolate to share with our coffee. Just a quick sugar hit to get us moving for the afternoon.

It was a fabulous job which consumed a lot of energy, yet we certainly didn't eat to support stamina and endurance. We were eating to support obesity and lethargy and on the whole, we encouraged each other all the way to lead unhealthy lifestyles. The workload was often so overwhelming; I think we all sought a little time out as well as comfort in the fast food we were consuming.

For a while, these fatty foods didn't seem to affect my weight or even my health to any great extent but after about a year in this environment, my very slim frame shifted to a more curvaceous shape. The women in our family have been blessed with ample busts, small waists and plenty of curves. I seemed to get an extra dose of roundness in the rear end as well. Focussing on my weight wasn't really important to me back then. Doing a really impressive job for the company, wearing fantastic clothes and going out to clubs and pubs with my fab friends was really my main priority in life.

In the midst of all this routine, I was contacted by my modelling agency for an upcoming audition. A really big fashion show was casting models for this event where lots of wonderful designers were going to be showcasing their new collections. It was going to be a show stopping extravaganza and I definitely wanted to participate. These shows were just so much fun, getting to wear designer clothes, modelling to fabulous music, lots of lights, cameras and air kissing; it was exciting. Audition day came and I can clearly remember the panel of four co-ordinators selecting the models over a two week period for the show.

When it was my turn to sashay down the runway, I stepped out onto the catwalk with complete confidence. I got my best blue steel look going on and I worked it on the runway. The designers were smiling at me and I felt pretty confident that I was going to be selected. I normally always made it through these auditions successfully, so why would this day be any different. As I turned around to head back down the catwalk, one of the co-ordinators of the event said loudly to another co-ordinator on the panel, "Oh, her bum is *quite* big don't you think? It's possibly too big for the show!" I thought, *Oh my god, are they talking about my bottom?* Was there someone else on the runway that I didn't see? I turned my head discreetly and glanced down at my butt. *It's not that big,* I thought. I was horrified. It was customary to never ever leave a catwalk without turning around and facing the audience with one final pose, as it was quite simply bad manners to exit without that last turn. I was just about at the end of my walk; my face was flushed and burning from embarrassment. I took a deep breath and I slowly turned around and smiled glamorously at the panel. Inside, my confidence and bottom had been obviously affected, but I never for one minute allowed anyone to witness what I was really feeling.

Before I left the catwalk, the co-ordinator that pointed out my huge rear end said to me, "If you can shift a bit of weight from your behind by next week, come back and audition again and you will probably get in." I acknowledged her comment and walked off. My throat was tight and my face felt flushed but I kept telling myself, *You're ok, you're ok* and with that, me and my enormous butt left the building! At first I was completely demoralised, but by the time I had got home I was actually feeling sorry for the woman's tactlessness and inability to be discreet. She had quite openly judged my ability to participate in the show based on the size of my backside and she seemed to take great pleasure in doing so.

Now, I realised it was a fashion show so body shape was paramount to the criteria, but I had met the sizing requirements and my portfolio shots had been selected by this particular panel. My measurements were there for all to see; bust, waist and hips. If I really was unsuitable because of my generous derriere, why not just say thankyou and we will let you know and then just break it to me gently without the 'big butt' feedback.

I decided much to everyone's amazement that my bottom and I were going to re-audition the following week regardless. I no longer needed to *get* the job, but I did need to go back out there despite this woman's remark and 'strut my stuff', because after all, I was a size ten! This was one of the size requirements for the job and because I was a curvier size ten, I was told to lose it or lose out. This just wasn't acceptable to me. When would people acknowledge that we are not all stick thin and that women come in all shapes and sizes? A size ten bottom is not offensive, nor is it too big!

My friends thought I was absolutely insane to go back for a second round of verbal abuse on my bum and of course I was the butt of many a joke amongst my friends and co-workers. It was my opinion that by going back again I was taking a stand for all women who were curvy. My audition had taken on a whole new meaning. The fashion, the glamour; it had all pretty much gone by the wayside.

I didn't diet that week to prepare and actually I didn't even give a second thought to what I ate. In fact I went out the weekend prior to the next round of auditions and drank champagne with my girlfriends and danced up a storm at a local night club. I was shaking my butt like Beyoncé. On the day of the second round of auditions, I decided to just dress differently. Last audition I wore a cream dress which had a band of cream silk ribbon around the hip area. I loved that dress and wore it purely because it was so beautiful and was my absolute favourite. This time round, I wore a slimline black dress that was really fitted. It quite possibly accentuated my voluptuous bottom and womanly curves even more than the week before. As I anxiously waited in line for my turn to walk the runway, a hint of anger surged upwards in my throat when I spotted the *CURVY BUM* detective sitting on the panel at the end of the catwalk.

There were about three people in front of me waiting to audition. As I waited in line, I felt really nervous about stepping out again. I turned to the beautiful girl behind me and said to her, "Can I ask you a question? Does my bum look big in this?" She stepped back, glanced down at my derriere and said "Oh no, not at all. You look fantastic. I wish I had a lovely shape like you. I am so thin, I look like a guy!" I thanked her and reassured her that she did not look like a boy and that she was beautiful. She was about 5 feet 11 inches and had the face of an angel. As I stepped out onto that catwalk, I won't deny it, I was shaking in my designer heels but I looked directly into the bum detective's eyes and commenced my walk. It's so interesting isn't it that one person's comments can *make or break* your self-confidence. It takes a great deal of courage to stand up for yourself, especially if you feel bullied in some way. I decided to add just a little more swing to my walk that day as I figured if I was going to be rejected, I was going to flaunt my femininity and be proud of my shape.

I got to the end of the runway, turned around to walk back and waited for someone to yell out, "Hey, that's the bum from last week, remember; the big one?" As I waited for some acknowledgement, one of the panel members said, "Fantastic, you are through. Please make your way to room three to get your fittings done."

I am not sure what the deciding factor was that got me selected for the show. My bottom was the same size as the week prior and I drew even more attention to it this time around. Perhaps it was my attitude that screamed, *HERE I AM! I AM WOMAN, HEAR ME ROAR*. Maybe it was that *SASHA FIERCE* look on my face that said *I am confident and beautiful in my own skin* that magically made all the difference.

Until the 'bum detective' yelled out for the entire world to hear that my bum was too big, I had never really seen a problem with my curves. I actually loved them. My body had been faulty in regards to how it reacted to certain substances, but I rarely viewed myself unkindly. Quite frankly, I decided that she had the issue, not me and I was determined to prove a point, that point being, no-one has the right to demoralise you. Your body shape does not measure your personality, your spirit, your beauty or your heart. Words are powerful things that can either destroy, uplift or empower. We all have a choice in regards to what words we use on a daily basis. Be mindful of your language not only to yourself, but also to others.

To this day, I have taken my very valuable experiences, including the one I have just shared with you and I remain committed to reminding as many women who will listen to embrace their beauty in all its forms. You can turn any negative situation into a positive one. Don't allow someone else to determine your self-worth. If someone criticises you unjustly, it is their issue, not yours. Be assured, you are beautiful. Remind yourself every day that you are a work of art and walk with pride through this world. Confidence is one of the most beautiful qualities you can possess. There are many facets to beauty and what makes a person beautiful. Beauty comes from the heart and the soul and it is often indescribable. Self-awareness and self-acceptance of our so called imperfections is where we find our true beauty.

"The beauty of a woman is not in a facial mode but the true beauty in a woman is reflected in her soul. It is the caring that she lovingly gives and the passion that she shows. The beauty of a woman grows with the passing years."
—Audrey Hepburn

Chapter Three

John & Yoko

Let's fast forward a few years now to when I met my husband-to-be in my early twenties. It was an instant connection and we began living together almost immediately. I had collided with the person that I wanted to share my world with, so it was natural to instantly cohabitate. At this point, I was working on many a major fashion parade and socially, life was party after party. He was managing a night club in Perth so if you can imagine combining my lifestyle with his lifestyle, it was a recipe for a health and wellness disaster.

Late nights that extended into early mornings, bad food, plenty of alcohol and parties; it doesn't take a rocket scientist to work out that the focus was on having an absolutely fabulous time at every opportunity. In my early twenties, I was easily influenced and late nights, lots of champagne and bad food became simply a way of life. The week days and nights were hectic and fast-paced. By Friday and Saturday night, the work load and commitments were at their peak and working through until dawn Sunday was normal. Truth be told, we actually worked through till midnight and after we had completed our workload, we partied till dawn Sunday.

Sunday soon became a day of recovery, the day we rested. We had to rest as we were always so hung-over and exhausted. We formally declared Sundays to be the traditional and official day of rest and worship. Typically, we took that rest and worship thing to a whole new level. We rested alright; we didn't even get out of bed. We worshipped alright; we worshipped home delivery take-away food and unhealthy treats all day long. It became a weekly tradition that Sunday would be spent resting, recovering and eating. I have discovered over the years that I do not seem to have an 'OFF' button and that my gauge that determines fullness and excessive consumption of food and alcohol is faulty. To this day, I have to be aware of my ability to over indulge. Whether it's food, wine or celebrating; I am an over achiever.

On one of these particular Sundays, while we were lying in bed with the TV on, surrounded by blueberry croissant crumbs and empty potato chip wrappers, a documentary came on about John Lennon and Yoko Ono. The footage showed John and Yoko lying in a white, low-set double bed under two huge glass windows. There were these massive cardboard signs above their bed saying 'hair peace' and 'bed peace'. John and Yoko were actually staging what they called a bed-in for peace. These bed-ins were intended to represent a non-violent protest against war and they were an interesting way to draw attention towards promoting world peace, according to John Lennon. John and Yoko would lie in bed for up to two weeks and invite the press to listen to them talk about life, love and how to change the world. We were watching this footage intensely, slightly amused as to how similar the images on TV were to our own personal traditional Sunday bed-in. Even the bed and the room that John and Yoko were staging their love fest in were almost identical to our bedroom. There were only a couple of differences, one being that my husband-to-be wasn't a talented poet-singing-song-writer genius from the Beatles and I wasn't a petite multimedia artist and peace activist married to a superstar. The other difference was that John and Yoko were drawing attention to spreading peace. We were actually drawing attention to our ever increasing waistlines.

We were so shocked at the similarities that we officially declared our Sundays to be formally named 'The John and Yoko day'. On this day, we would eat a lot of unhealthy food, watch videos and stay in bed all day long. John and Yoko day became the most celebrated day of the week and the concept of this day spread like wildfire throughout the apartment building we lived in. We had made many friends in the complex and when they had invited us to dinner or drinks on a Sunday, obviously we had to decline due to our commitment to John and Yoko day. All of our friends simply loved the concept of our Sunday bed-ins and soon, it seemed like everyone in the Delamere Avenue high rise were staging their own private bed-ins. We had started an epidemic and a very unhealthy one at that!

It soon became evident one Monday morning after one of our bed-ins that I could no longer fit into any of my work clothes. I have what I call an exploding waistline; one minute you are eating what you like and everything is fine, you are cruising along and feeling fabulous and then BOOM, everything just bursts out from everywhere. It has never been a gradual process for me. I normally go to bed one size and then wake up a couple of sizes larger the next morning.

John Lennon, sorry, I mean my husband-to-be Tony and I had got engaged during these heady days of peace, love and croissants. My summer wedding was only four months away but somehow this important event must have slipped my mind as I lay in my bed on Sundays singing *Imagine* whilst chowing down fish and chips. I felt slightly panicked one particular morning when I tried on my gorgeous cream satin wedding gown with the sparkly tulle overlay and I could no longer zip it up. This was a crisis, it was an emergency as I hadn't just gained a couple of kilograms; I had gained around six. I had to do something drastic, so all impending bed-ins had to be cancelled. The infamous John and Yoko day was no more.

I swung into action that morning, as you do when your wedding dress is gaping about half a metre wide in the back. How was I to fit into my sparkling gown without giving up blueberry croissants and bubbles? What a dilemma. I decided I would just reduce the amount of bad food and champers and run around the block a few times, that ought to get me back into shape; it had always worked before. I did lose weight but I still couldn't quite get that zip up on my gown a week prior to my big day, so I just didn't really eat anything in the lead up to the wedding. I had no problems fitting into my dress on my wedding day but I was tired, I had little energy and I certainly didn't feel like a blushing bride.

We had booked a private suite at a beautiful hotel overlooking the beach for our honeymoon. We had access to free drinks and beautiful food 24/7 on this exclusive floor of the hotel and we made the most of it. By the end of our honeymoon, I had pretty much regained half of the weight I had lost. I wasn't concerned, I had been enjoying the most amazing week and really that was all I cared about.

I felt invincible in my twenties; I think most of us feel this way at that age. I didn't think of my health or the fact that I was laying the foundation for an even bigger struggle with my weight and my body for the rest of my life. I have known hundreds of women who have yo-yo dieted just as I did and I am well aware of how damaging extreme dieting can be. There is so much conflicting information available about how to lose weight and branded diets are a multi-billion dollar industry. Sustaining some of the diets available today is nearly impossible. I can assure you, there is absolutely no quick fix or no magic pill that will achieve long term sustainable weight management. I know, I have tried to find one but it doesn't exist. If your weight goes up and down constantly, quit the fad dieting. Instead educate yourself about the benefits of clean healthy eating and daily exercise. Eating healthily every day, as well as moving is the best way to achieve a healthy body. Make the commitment to embrace healthy eating as a lifestyle; take an oath to avoid the diet trap. If you keep searching for a quick fix for weight loss, you will never achieve optimum good health and wellness in all its glory.

Do you ever think about extreme dieting and the damage it does to your body? Extreme dieting can cause serious health issues. A massive reduction in calories may give you short term weight loss, but it will drastically slow down your metabolism and may also reduce your muscle mass. Along with this, your body will be deprived of the vital vitamins, minerals and nutrients it so desperately needs to function. Self-care as well as devoting time and energy to your own health is the best way to achieve wellness. How you live, what you eat and what your mind is focussed on thought-wise really does determine your weight, your health and your life.

Well, I may have fitted into my dress only just on my wedding day, but what I didn't realise was that I was laying down the foundation for an even bigger struggle than just getting that zip done up for years to come.

"Most people have no idea how good their body is designed to feel."
—Kevin Trudeau

Chapter Four

The Visitor

While I was growing up, I would sometimes hear my mum and nana talking in hushed tones about a mysterious visitor. I remember hearing them talk about this visitor like he was some kind of dangerous axe murderer. Their voices were always low and serious and if you walked into the room mid-discussion, they would quickly stop talking and change the subject. It was quite terrifying really. I imagined the visitor to be some evil character and quite honestly, I had envisaged the visitor to be a tall, dark, creepy thin man wearing a big hat and a black cape. I figured he caused all sorts of harm and was extremely dangerous. At night, when I would go to bed, I would lay there with my eyes wide open in the dark fearful that the visitor might appear and attack me.

My worst fears were confirmed one afternoon on returning from school. My older sister was holed up in her room crying in pain and sobbing hysterically. She was visibly upset and distressed and Mum came out of her room and said, "Leave your sister to rest". I asked, "What's wrong with her?" Mum replied, "Oh nothing" and then as she walked off I heard her mumble something about *the visitor.* Well, that just confirmed my reasons to be fearful. That visitor obviously had somehow got into our house and attacked my sister and I couldn't understand why Mum hadn't called the police. It was very clear to me that Mum was perhaps scared of the visitor and feared for her own safety.

I finally learnt who that visitor was when I was around twelve years old. I realised that the visitor was just Mum and Nana's code word for your period. It came as a shock to me in more ways than one as I screamed in agony when I had my first visit from the visitor. As I lay in my bed doubled up with cramps, I could hear my mum talking to Nana in a low voice, "Jo has her visitor". I remember hearing Nana respond with, "Oh dear."

I had finally met the visitor and the experience was every bit as horrendous as I had imagined. I soon started to experience cramping, migraines and mood swings, as so many women do and as I got older these symptoms intensified. Fast forward from the first visit from the visitor to my twenties and the lead up to my period was like travelling on a train that had derailed and was spiralling out of control.

My patience for my partner and anyone basically on the planet on a scale from one to ten was zero. In one hour I could experience sixty different emotions and I didn't even know that there were sixty different emotions. I could look at my beloved, the person I was about to share my whole life with and in one breath I would experience this massive wave of deep love for him, so intense it was overwhelming. In the next breath, had he perhaps just looked at me the wrong way, that feeling of deep love turned to absolute distaste. Then I would flip back to love. Imagine, I love you, I hate you, I love you, I hate you and all the while I would be thinking, perhaps this is not premenstrual syndrome, maybe this is just my personality.

I had to have two wardrobes. One was stocked with gorgeous clothes for weeks one to three of the month, the other was stocked with oversized t-shirts and track pants two sizes above my standard size. This was the attire worn during my *visitor*. I would retain so much fluid and feel so bloated and heavy, that in itself was enough to declare that in my next life, if there was one, I was returning as a man. My hair would become greasy, my skin would break out, I was lethargic and craved chocolate by the bucketful. I couldn't watch an episode of *Highway to Heaven* without sobbing uncontrollably. I didn't even recognise myself during my monthly encounters with the visitor. I would swing, fly, fall and flounder during this week every month as I battled pain, anxiety, weight gain and excruciatingly heavy periods. The fourth week of every month was circled on the calendar as a warning to all those who shared my world as a time to prepare for storms, hail and more than likely destructive winds.

My PMS symptoms were heightened because of my relatively unhealthy lifestyle. I was taking evening primrose oil by the truck load as it helped relieve PMS and also helped with mood swings but really, I was counteracting their goodness with all of my other little vices. My diet was just not clean enough and my body made me well aware that it was not happy with how

I treated it. My bad diet amplified the intensity of my horrible symptoms.

I am not sure why, but just prior to the onset of my visitor, I would always have a huge problem with my ability to speak intelligently and rationally. One minute, I would be speaking calmly and with clarity and then the next minute I would be ranting and raving like a lunatic. I have found that my actual words quite easily shoot out of my mouth unintentionally muddled up and even backwards. I am normally efficient and organised, but during the visitor's onset, I have been known to place my mobile phone in the freezer whilst unpacking groceries. I have attempted to try and enter the apartment three floors directly under my apartment thinking it was my place, (I got out on the 8th floor and not the 11th floor) and I have even taken on man-handling a feared bikie member for not paying his bill, when I was managing a hotel that he had illegally checked his way into. These actions were all under the influence of the visitor.

Memory loss, confusion, fuzziness, heaviness, irritability, these monthly symptoms really forced me to arrange my life schedule according to the visitor. Week four of the month was a total write-off; if only I knew then what I know now about the impact of lifestyle on the body during the menstrual cycle, I certainly could have managed my symptoms more effectively. I spent years searching for relief from PMS and yet I never once examined clean eating, meditation and exercise as a possible way of reducing the severity of the problems I was having.

How do you aggravate and heighten PMS symptoms? Eat plenty of refined sugars, carbohydrates, sweets, chocolate, ice cream, pre-packaged foods and fatty take-outs. Then to increase the intensity of those mood swings, irritability and energy highs and lows, be sure to stuff yourself with white bread, white rice and white flour. This will ensure that your already inflamed system reaches maximum inflammation overload. Don't even consider going for a walk to relieve those painful cramps, hell no! Just lay on the lounge and focus on the intensity of the pain; that ought to do it! All these things actually help create that painful, pro-inflammatory environment.

There is no definitive answer as to why some women suffer PMS worse than others. I do know I come from a long line of women who have been challenged by the visitor. We can trivialise PMS, make jokes about it, but the reality is that it can significantly impact on your life if you suffer from severe premenstrual syndrome. There are definite lifestyle steps that you can take every day to improve the severity of these symptoms. For example, eating a clean fresh diet full of fruit and vegetables, lean healthy protein and healthy fats is a great place to start. Eliminate caffeine and replace coffee with water and herbal tea. Reducing your salt intake to decrease bloating is a major step forward and up the ante on your physical activity. A good brisk walk is a great coping mechanism for period cramps. There is evidence to show that calcium can also improve symptoms of PMS, so whether you increase your intake of calcium rich foods or look at supplements to include daily, consider calcium as a definite support to PMS. Don't under-estimate the power of meditation, yoga and rest as a way of bringing peace to an aggravated body. These beautiful practices will enrich your health, enhance wellness and will bring balance back to the mind, body and spirit.

So my visitor has made regular visits for almost 40 years. Had I realised our association was going to be so lengthy and intense, I would have put into place some really serious rules from day one to ensure that I was more in control of the challenges associated with these visits. Remember, you are in control of your body. Yes, we face challenges, imbalances and struggles, some of us more than others, but take full responsibility for your health through a clean diet, exercise, meditation and whatever practices bring peace and balance to your system. No matter what health issues you face, you can dramatically improve your ability to cope as well as the outcome by understanding that the mind, body and spirit are all interlinked. Treat each area with respect and nurture with self-love and you will find that your system will not act up in defiance.

"Everything in your life is a reflection of a choice you have made. If you want a different result, make a different choice."

—Author — unknown

Chapter Five

Womb service

When I was twenty nine, I fell pregnant with my son. The morning sickness was overwhelming and even to this day if anyone mentions the words 'morning sickness', I automatically feel that same awful sensation of nausea that I experienced during pregnancy. I was lucky really as it was only on rising until about 2pm that my dry retching, projectile vomiting and inability to rise from the bathroom floor occurred. As soon as the clock struck 2pm, as if by magic, my morning sickness would subside until the next day. I had morning sickness from my fourth week of pregnancy until my twelfth week.

I had friends who would fall pregnant and bask in this beautiful pregnancy glow. They would be simply illuminated. Their hair would magically become lustrous and would cascade down their shoulders like Rapunzel. Their bodies would slowly become more voluptuous, curvaceous and beautiful and their skin would be luminous. They would transform into pregnant goddesses just revelling in pregnancy bliss, but I didn't experience that same sensation. I was too busy driving the porcelain bus each morning in my pyjamas so even getting dressed was an issue.

I actually knew the minute I fell pregnant and also instinctively knew that I was having a boy. You know how some women say they have no idea what sex their baby is when they are pregnant? Well, I knew straight away; I had absolutely no doubt in my mind. Even during my extreme nausea in those first twelve weeks, I knew my baby was a little boy. I found out I was pregnant when I was living on a tropical island with my husband. I threw up under pretty much every palm tree on this island paradise and as it was fairly remote, we decided to relocate back to Western Australia to be closer to family as we awaited the birth of our baby.

At week thirteen, my morning sickness stopped. I remember gingerly getting out of bed and placing my feet on the floor in readiness for throwing up and I was elated when I actually felt fine. I glanced in the mirror. It had been weeks since I had been able to stand upright for long, as I had spent most of this period on the bathroom floor and had never quite made it up as high as the mirror to see how I was faring. When I finally looked at myself, I was horrified. Where was my pregnancy glow I wondered? My hair was like straw, I was pale and had dark circles under my eyes and I looked like I hadn't slept in weeks. I must admit, I was a bit confused as I had always assumed that women flourished during pregnancy. The magazines I had skipped through in the doctor's surgery showed pregnant women all beautifully groomed as they smiled angelically, whilst resting their perfectly manicured hands on their tiny little baby bumps.

Well, it was only week thirteen, so maybe my pregnancy beauty would start to kick in soon. I had stopped feeling sick *just like that*, so perhaps I would wake up the next day and my hair would have changed from straw to silk and I would have turned into a goddess as well. First things first though. It was time to get out of those pyjamas that I had been wearing for weeks and get into some springtime fashion. The weather was gorgeous and I was feeling better, so it was time to go swimming, walking and really get into looking after myself. I went to my closet and pulled out some really nice navy linen shorts to wear. I was going to team them with a lovely soft white, cotton top which would be perfect for a stroll along the beach. I pulled on those shorts and tried to zip them up. Here I was, faced with my next challenge; my shorts no longer fitted me. The harder I tried to do them up, the more difficult it became.

My pregnant belly had started to emerge. How could this be? I had just thrown up for eight weeks and had lived on rice, water and tea. I was only just thirteen weeks' pregnant for heaven's sake. All my goddess-like friends had told me that they hadn't started showing or even gaining weight until six or seven months into their pregnancies. I was just three months pregnant and already I couldn't do my pants up. OH MY GOD, what next? Was it not enough that I had literally dragged myself through this first trimester? Wasn't thirteen weeks too early to be showing? Maybe I was having twins and one baby had hidden during the ultrasound. It was far too soon to shop for maternity clothes in my opinion. If I was already showing at thirteen weeks, what would I be like at full term? I was starting to get nervous. Never mind I thought, suck it up and get on with it. There had to be something in my wardrobe that would fit.

While searching for something to wear that morning, I was overwhelmed by this incredible urge to eat. I hadn't eaten much for weeks and then within minutes, I was ravenous. I quickly forgot about the clothing dilemma as the issue at hand was to get to a kitchen, a fridge, a pantry, or whatever to satisfy this unbelievable need to eat. I had seen the send-ups on TV of pregnant women sending their husbands out at 2am in the morning for pickles, chocolate and ice-cream but I had always thought that was just nonsense. I had never imagined for one minute that those scenarios could be real.

My cravings kicked in pretty quickly; I wanted to eat savoury food. When a craving would come, it would be really intense. Whatever I was imagining, I could taste it and even smell it throughout every cell in my body. The cravings were so strong; I swear I would have climbed a mountain even in my underwear to get to a supermarket to satisfy these urges. The cravings were often confusing. Have you ever been to a restaurant with an incredibly enticing menu and you don't know what to order? You open up the menu and there are so many choices that you want to try it all. Imagine my scenario: I will order the Cajun chicken. Oh yes, that sounds great, right? Oh, but what about that delectable fried rice and the vegetable dim sums? Why don't you order that as well? Did you want fries with your order madam? Would you like a burger with your dim sums? How about we stop off and pick you up a packet of potato crisps and smash them up and then sprinkle them over your fried rice for some extra crunch? Sounds crazy doesn't it?

It was so confusing and yet so overpowering. I had lost all control yet again! All signs indicated that my little baby boy was just chilling out on a bean bag in my womb playing on a PlayStation, all the while tossing up whether to eat at The Happy Dragons Chinese Garden Restaurant or grab a Happy Meal from McDonalds. I developed massive cravings for the cereal Nutrigrain and was literally eating it by the truck load. Interestingly enough, I tolerated that cereal really well during pregnancy which is strange as it contains wheat, oatmeal and gluten which are all ingredients that I usually react to. I also fancied beer, but I don't drink beer. I never indulge in beer, but during pregnancy it took me all my time not to rip open a Foster's lager and wash down my cereal with it, I wanted to drink beer so badly.

Pregnancy was a struggle for me that's for sure. I certainly wasn't blooming with that mum-to-be radiance that everyone had told me about. At seventeen weeks though, after all my nausea, vomiting, cravings, fatigue and general nutty outbursts, finally I was rewarded with the most precious experience. I will never forget this particular day when my husband and I decided to spend the day at the beach. It was a warm, sunny beautiful Perth day. I was excited about heading out into the sunshine, swimming in the Indian Ocean and just relaxing. I knocked over a carton of Nutrigrain before we headed out, popped on my best 'Pamela Anderson Baywatch' red swimsuit and off we went. My husband dug a little hole in the sand so I could lie down and sunbake comfortably on my tummy and positioned it perfectly so my pregnant belly would just fit nicely in the hole. I was so comfortable and relaxed and so off he went down to the pier to fish, leaving me to rest. I was lying peacefully enjoying the warmth of the sun when all of a sudden, I felt this really strong fluttering sensation in my belly; I could feel my baby moving. It continued to happen and each time it got a little bit stronger. I was so excited I stood up and ran all the way to the pier to let my husband know. I will never ever forget that day or that first movement. As long as I live, I will remember and treasure that feeling and the connection I had felt to my son.

At twenty-five weeks pregnant, I was having morning tea with my sister and my mum at a beachside café. I had felt a little sick that particular morning and my belly felt very heavy and uncomfortable, so I was feeling a bit strange and out of sorts. I took a quick bathroom break halfway through our get-together and I was horrified to see that I had started to experience some bleeding. I panicked and raced out to my mum and we contacted my doctor, who insisted I head straight to the hospital where I was quickly admitted and forced to stay in bed to rest and be monitored. Although the doctors couldn't pinpoint the cause of the bleeding, they did prepare me for the possibility of losing my baby if things did not settle. I remember thinking, *No way! That is just not an option.*

I was confined to bed in the hospital while they monitored me constantly. I was terrified of losing my precious baby. I lay flat out in the bed and for most of the day I would visualise a big angel standing over me with a vacuum cleaner; not your regular old Hoover, but a grand, gold, vacuum cleaner! I have always had faith in the power of positive thinking, so I had nothing to lose by letting my mind focus on visualising a miracle. The angel would take that vacuum and magically make it pass through my stomach to where my baby was. The angel would then vacuum away anything around the womb that was threatening to cause harm and I would close my eyes and see my baby all curled up safely inside this protected area. I would visualise that vacuum thoroughly removing any debris potentially targeting the womb and watch this event happening in my mind's eye, until I could see nothing in that area but beautiful crystal-clear water surrounding my son. I literally did this visualisation exercise every day while I was in hospital. Each day the bleeding got less and less and each time I did the visualisation exercise, I would hear the angel say, *there are no threats, it's all fine.* By day twelve of my hospital stay, the bleeding had stopped and I was allowed to go home. The doctor said to me as I had my discharge check-up, "You are very lucky. Go home and rest until this baby is born." I wondered was it bed rest and good doctors, or an angel with a vacuum that got me discharged?

I was certainly nervous when I got home, fearful I would start bleeding again, but I kept up my miraculous angel visualisation every day until my son was born. Even his grand entrance into the world was challenging. I was induced at forty-one weeks, exhausted and heavy but excited about meeting my son. My water was broken at 7am and I was fully dilated by 9am. I was relieved when my doctor informed me that my baby would be here in the blink of an eye. I was advised that I was going to have a quick birth but things became complicated. The contractions had turned into just one huge contraction and my baby boy was not interested in venturing out. It turned out that bub was in what is called the 'occiput posterior foetal position'. This OP position is when the back of baby's head is against the mother's back looking up. It was not an ideal way to enter the world by any means, so after one long contraction that lasted six hours when the doctors realised that my son was facing the wrong way, he was swiftly assisted to make his entrance by use of a vacuum extraction. I was definitely hoping the guardian angel that had assisted me while in hospital, was on hand to now assist with the delivery. It was an exhausting labour although relatively quick, as it took just nine hours before he made his grand entrance. All the drama and pain was swiftly forgotten when I heard my baby's cry and cradled him in my arms.

After his arrival, we spent another week in hospital while he was treated with light therapy for newborn jaundice. By the time we took our son home, I was an exhausted, hormonal mess. Once we had settled in, fatigue and the overwhelming challenge of becoming a new mum hit. I struggled with breast feeding and my energy levels were very low. I was tired, teary and naturally extremely over-protective of my newborn and it took me a few months to feel somewhat normal and establish any sort of routine. Having a new baby is joyous, exciting, overwhelming and exhausting; well, that's how I remember it!

The sheer emotional rollercoaster ride I experienced after my son's birth was challenging to say the least. One minute I was consumed with this unexplainable love for this tiny human being and then in the next minute, I was in tears from lack of sleep. I remember being bombarded with advice from well-meaning friends and relatives on what I should be doing during the first few weeks of motherhood. Don't hold him this way, burp him that way, he is too hot, he is too cold. Don't give him a dummy, give him a dummy. Don't do this, don't do that. Haven't you lost weight yet? You should be back to your pre baby body! What are you eating? Should you be consuming that? If being a new mum wasn't challenging enough, the endless advice and critiquing certainly added to the confusion and exhaustion that accompanied those first few months. If I could write a letter to myself at age twenty-nine when I had just become a mum, it would read something like this —

Dear Jo,

Well done YOU. Go you good thing. Did you ever imagine that you could create such a gorgeous, beautiful boy? Not every woman is blessed with this gift, so be sure to give thanks. He is healthy and that is the most important thing. Don't waste one single second on worrying about the housework, the washing, the fact that you are still in your PJs and it is 3pm. Those dreadlocks you are now sporting from not brushing your hair, they really suit you. Only you could pull off that Rastafarian look with such ease.

Try and rest when he is resting. Nurture your little boy, but don't forget to nurture yourself. All that conflicting advice you are getting, let it wash over you. Do what you feel is best. Listen to your own intuition when you are challenged and if all else fails, phone your mum. This time will go so very fast. Enjoy your precious little baby. Spend more time looking at his gorgeous face and less time stressing because before you know it, he will be twenty-one. You will be hard pressed to cradle him in your arms again the way you can today, plus that would be awkward and extremely embarrassing for him.

Nurture your body during this time. Choose healthier food, Jo. Don't just grab a piece of toast when you can, prioritise. You are more important than the washing and the housework. Pay careful attention to your diet as you will feel so much better if you do. You will recover faster and you will feel like your old self sooner than later. Motherhood is challenging; it doesn't come with a how-to manual, so do what you feel is best always.

Take better care of yourself, Jo. Pace yourself. Set realistic goals to achieve wellness. Eat healthy, clean, sensible meals and get fresh air and sunshine every day. Walk with your baby and rest with your baby. Your body will soon return to a healthy weight at its own pace. Did you ever imagine that your body could even do what it just did? It is just miraculous really.

You are worth taking care of, so do not neglect your own health. Anyway, you will need to muster up all your strength now for when he turns two and starts defying you, but that's another letter.

With love to myself.

From that day forward, I realised how incredibly amazing our bodies are. To carry and bring a child into this world is truly a miracle and a privilege.

"Giving birth and being born brings us into the essence of creation, where the human spirit is courageous and bold and the body, a miracle of wisdom.
—Harriette Hartigan

Chapter Six

You have the fat gene

I think we have clearly established the fact that I have spent a great deal of my life battling with my body and going up and down with my weight. It's never been balanced and even at my healthiest and sleekest, it seemed that I had to work a whole lot harder than most to maintain what is considered a normal healthy body size.

In my thirties, I finally achieved that perfect size ten again. It was a monumental effort to get it and although I felt fantastic physically at this size, it always felt like underneath this shape, there was a voluptuous curvy woman bursting at the seams. It was as if I had achieved the shape I wanted, but internally, every part of my DNA was screaming, *LET ME OUT*. As I said, it felt wonderful to be a size ten, but I just didn't quite fit into it. I felt like if I breathed out, my curves would explode outwards and if curves had a voice, they would go, *YES, we are free*!

I was working in a medical cosmetic clinic some years ago as a wellness consultant. One day the clinical director had suggested we go to Melbourne and learn about DNA testing and how it influences our weight and overall wellness. The clinical director was very slim and had an appetite like a horse. When I first met her, I thought that perhaps she had worms. She could pack a lot of food away and she never gained an ounce. If I shared a meal with her, I would pick and fuss over something that was gluten free, wheat free and low in calories. She would order absolutely anything that took her fancy and when she was finished, she would proceed to eat the leftovers on my plate. Somehow, the calories she consumed seemed to end up on my hips. As if by magic, I would gain two kilos watching her eat.

As part of the course, we had to have our own DNA tested. Our genes impact on every aspect of our life, from nutrition and disease, to fitness and even how we function. If you understand your DNA, it can help you to identify your personal challenges. You can then manage these challenges to improve your overall goals with health and wellness.

The clinical director did my DNA test. She swabbed the side of my mouth, packaged up my saliva and sent it off to the lab for testing. We went to Melbourne to complete the DNA testing lectures and we were pretty excited about participating in this workshop. On the first day, within about thirty minutes after the lecturer began, I was pretty sure that this course was being delivered in Swahili as I did not understand one word that was being said. I looked at my colleague sitting next to me and she too looked confused. I saw her searching for the

'Google translator' on her phone, so obviously she did not understand Swahili either.

I did pick up the words FTO gene during the training; this gene is apparently linked to obesity and diabetes. "I definitely have that one," I said to my colleague. It was a tough course that's for sure and its complicated delivery made it even more overwhelming.

Basically, we inherit our make-up, our beautiful qualities as well as those qualities we see as faults from our beloved families. Each cell in the human body contains about 25,000 to 35,000 genes. These genes carry information that go towards determining our traits which are characteristics we inherit from our parents. I have inherited my dad's fair Irish skin, his love of potatoes and red wine, his wicked sense of humour and I think I got his manly shaped legs as well. I'm not sure what that gene is called, all I know is I don't need a DNA test to confirm it! These traits are all rather endearing and attractive on Dad who is one devilishly handsome man, but on me, well, think about it. The wicked sense of humour I am grateful for; the legs, potato addiction and the red wine drinking sit slightly differently on me than they do on him.

It can take up to three months before the results of your DNA are analysed and finally, after about twelve weeks, my test results arrived. Apparently, I have the fat gene, the gene that is associated with addiction, the gene that is associated with diabetes, the gene that causes you to engage in risky behaviour and also the gene that if you drink too much coffee, you can just drop dead!

I already knew that collecting a saliva sample and testing my DNA would only confirm what I already knew. If you look at my DNA report in print, it could easily be interpreted as tragic, as it portraits me as a skydiving, booze-fuelled, hyperactive person who runs on coffee. The footnote on the bottom of the report should read: 'It is highly recommended that you check yourself into a rehabilitation centre for the genetically challenged before you expire from too much caffeine, heart failure, diabetes and obesity.' This DNA test really indicates that I am so genetically challenged that it would not be unreasonable to witness me spiralling out of control at any tick of the clock. Swinging from a chandelier naked, whilst slamming down a gin and tonic, would obviously be seen as normal behaviour for me.

Although the results of the test were bleak, I decided to look at this information as a special plan that actually allows me to manage potential health issues; a map so to speak where I could navigate my future health to a degree. I actually really appreciate my DNA, my unique traits, my little idiosyncrasies. Each and every one of them has taken me on a fantastic journey; a journey of self-discovery, a journey of experiences that are invaluable to me, a journey like no-one else's. My excessive consumption of coffee, that extra glass of vino, my skydiving adventures and my low blood sugar are all just a part of what makes me, well, kind of interesting!

As with every single aspect of my life, I choose to view each trait that I have inherited as a positive, wonderful part of my incredible uniqueness. Now that I am aware of these genes, I can manage my choices better to avoid that potential heart attack or trip to Alcoholics Anonymous. The thing is, we are all uniquely different and that is what makes us especially beautiful. If we set unrealistic expectations for our bodies, we can sometimes do more damage than good. I may have the fat gene, I may have also inherited some of my mother's beautiful, womanly curves, I may also have inherited dad's sense of humour; this somehow should be celebrated.

Beauty and confidence extend far beyond your face and your body shape. It starts from within and encompasses many things – energy, personality, life force. It is not all about what size we are or what shape we are. It's a combination of many different aspects of you that make you uniquely beautiful. That having been said, we can all make a difference as to how we feel and to our energy levels when we respect our bodies with healthy nutrition and regular exercise. We need to stop comparing ourselves to other women and instead stand proud and acknowledge our own individual beauty. What makes a woman truly beautiful is when she is comfortable and confident in her own skin. It is at this point, you absolutely radiate a glow that is far too bright to ignore.

After I had digested my DNA results, I took some time to acknowledge who I actually inherited my genes from. My beautiful nana would occasionally clutch her chest and fall down onto the lounge and have to breathe deeply to bring her heartbeat back into rhythm. Perhaps I inherited that funny heart rhythm from her. If that is the case, I can't think of a more beautiful person to inherit it from. Nana was also curvaceous and fuller figured. If I have in fact inherited that FTO gene from Nana, well, once again I can't think of a sweeter person to inherit that one from either. Self-awareness and acceptance of our imperfections is where we find our absolute true beauty.

"There is a crack in everything, that's how the light gets in."
—Leonard Cohen

Chapter Seven

The change

Well, I thought I had pretty much experienced everything there was to experience as a woman – PMS, pregnancy, childbirth, being slim, being fuller figured. Surely, that was enough for one lifetime. My cup had runneth over in more ways than one.

I was still working in the same clinic consulting with clients on wellness. The clinic had recently introduced a medical body-shaping device that used low frequency ultrasound to target localised cellulite and fat. This incredible treatment was so effective it literally melted fatty deposits away. I was fortunate enough, along with some other staff, to learn how to operate the machine and perform the treatment. Firstly, I would educate the clients on healthy eating and if they were good candidates for the procedure, I would proceed to treat the fatty areas that they were aiming to reduce.

The most popular area to treat with this device was the stomach. It seemed that we had a consistent flow of women who just could not lose that belly fat. The device offered such astounding results with reducing fat in this area and more often than not, the reduction was instantaneous. It wasn't long before we had women lining up in their droves, bellies exposed, begging to be treated.

When the women were receiving their treatments, they were often so comfortable and relaxed, they would not only bare their stomachs to me, but they would also bare their souls. Massage therapists, hairdressers, beauticians alike, not only perform specialised treatments on clients, they are also unofficial councillors. This is an accepted part of the job and one that isn't included or recognised when you graduate. Clients share mainly their troubles and challenges with you when placed in that chair or on that table. My clients were very open with me and shared their most intimate details of what they hated about their bodies.

One particular morning, when I was getting ready for work at the clinic, I reached for one of my most favourite tops to wear. It was a beautiful pale blue, satin shirt which I loved. I went to do it up and it felt tight, in fact, I could barely do the buttons up. I had only worn it a few weeks before and I hadn't noticed any problems with it then. It was particularly tight around the middle area, but I didn't have a lot of time to think too much about it so I threw it off and found something else to wear.

Over the next few weeks, I noticed that my tops were getting tight, especially around my waist and mid-section. Despite all my curves and weight fluctuations over the years, I had always had a pretty small waist so this was weird. After writing up notes on my second client for the day, our amazingly talented receptionist at the clinic gave me my next client file and I confided in him about my expanding midriff dilemma. "I think I am melting away the stomach fat on these women and it is somehow transferring over to my stomach," I said. "My stomach is expanding day by day and I have no idea why!" He responded with, "How many vinos did you have last night, sweetie?"

I thought about it and I had consumed one glass of red wine with dinner; ok maybe two. I hadn't changed anything to do with my diet. I was still walking daily, but it was like someone was just pumping my stomach up bit by bit each day. With this expanding waistline, I also felt more fatigued than usual and really struggled with low energy. I would get into bed and toss and turn and would have these times where I felt like my skin was itching from the inside out. It was all so strange and unsettling.

My husband and I were out having a coffee one particular morning. I sat down to read the paper and as he headed towards me with our coffees, I saw him stop and chat to a woman at another table. I didn't recognise her at first, but he reminded me of where we both knew her from. He casually mentioned that she had said, "Oh yes, I saw Jo walk through before. Congratulations to you both. When is the baby due? What is she maybe four months pregnant?" He seemed horrified, but not as horrified as I was. I was just shy of turning fifty years of age and having a baby at fifty just didn't quite fit for us personally. The fact that she thought I was pregnant and I wasn't, mortified me! As I digested what she had said, I started to express my frustration and well, to be honest, I kind of lost it.

So, it went something like this: "WHAT, do I look pregnant? Do I? Well, do I?" I knew my stomach was expanding, but seriously? PREGNANT? My voice was getting louder at this point. My poor husband was trying to console me, then he had to pacify me, then he had to stop me from going over and confronting her. Then he kicked himself for telling me what she had said. I was venting, "How ridiculous. She knows I am not pregnant. She always had a thing for you. She is trying to make me look bad. Is she pregnant? SHE looks pregnant. Seriously! What is her problem?"

In ninja-like speed, my beautiful husband gathered me up and swiftly and gently guided me out of the coffee shop before my stomach and I came out all guns blazing. By the time we got home, I was reduced to a sobbing mess. "I don't know what is wrong with me. Maybe I am pregnant," I wailed. My husband said, "Umm NO. I don't think you are, darling. Remember, you can't have any more babies?" Oh yes, that was right. I definitely couldn't have another baby. It was physically impossible. I pulled myself together and decided that the 'Is Jo pregnant comment' was just this woman's way of being catty!

At that point in time, we were experiencing our winter and we were blessed with really cool evenings. They were perfect nights for sleeping, so I had heard. Well, if they were such perfect nights for slumber, why was I tossing and turning all night long? While my husband lay peacefully snoring all cosy and warm under the blankets, I tossed and turned and kept turning the air conditioner to high. "Aren't you hot?" I would ask. His answer was always, "No". I was just continuously feeling feverish. I wanted to rip my clothes off and if I could have jammed myself into our double-door fridge, I would have given it a go.

I was having dinner with friends one beautiful night and we were sitting outside on a balcony taking in the amazing views of the city we called home. I felt so hot. I said, "Isn't anyone else hot?" Everyone ignored me except for one of my older female friends. She smiled and nodded. It appeared to me that perhaps she knew something that I didn't, as she sat there chuckling to herself. I was fanning myself trying to cool down, while everyone was donning wraps and shrugs to keep warm. I said, "God, I have always got a fever lately, I'd best get to the doctor." I heard her chuckle again and I wondered what she was laughing at. It was like through her laughter she was secretly conveying the following message, *Sucked in, you are having hot flushes. Thank god I am not the only one.*

I think I had convinced myself that perhaps I was facing a serious health issue. Bloated stomach, feeling out of sorts, continual fever, emotional – these are all definite symptoms that warrant a health check-up. I did what I always do when faced with a crisis, I called Mum. I confided in Mum and shared my symptoms. Mum always knows what is wrong; she knows even before I call her. It's like we have an invisible cord that connects us, a lifeline. Even though I live on the other side of the country, that cord runs straight to me and connects to my heart. Distance and even time does not block this cord and as soon as there is a crisis, she gets a little tug on her heartstrings and she knows that something is wrong. Mum has this connection with all of her children and grandchildren.

So I am explaining my issues to Mum and after a long period of silence she asks me, "When did you last see your visitor?" I was like, what? Who? What visitor? And then I remembered. "Oh yes, *that* visitor." Good god, I had forgotten about the dreaded visitor, as it had been quite a while since the visitor had made an appearance.

Mum said, "Hot flushes, crawling skin, expanding middle, emotional, not sleeping, no visitor! It sounds to me like you are experiencing the *change*." "The what?" I said. She replied in the same tone as she used to describe the visitor all those years ago, her voice low, serious and conveying impending doom, "THE CHANGE". Actually, to be honest, Mum's tone was not unlike the late, great Hollywood actor Vincent Price's tone when he did the voice-over on Alice Cooper's album, *Welcome to my Nightmare*. "Oh my god," I said. "Do you mean menopause?" "Yes," she whispered, so no-one could hear. I couldn't believe it, after such a tumultuous relationship with my body for what had seemed like forever, I was about to be challenged yet again. This time it was the dreaded *change*. I had seen those *change* images like the pregnancy ones in the glossy mags in the doctor's surgery. You know, the ones where an attractive, slim grey-haired woman dressed in white slacks, wearing a white linen shirt with a white cardigan draped around her shoulders is standing in a field of daisies with her arms outstretched embracing the sunshine, the caption reading, "Menopause. What menopause?" Those images create a lot of pressure. I could never pull off that perfectly groomed, overly excited to be facing yet another challenge with my body, kind of look!

I made a time to see the doctor. As I dressed for my appointment, that image of the grey-haired lady re-appeared in my mind. Well, I thought, *if I am facing the change perhaps I need to also embrace the fact that I will no longer be shopping in those lovely little fashion shops for young women.* Maybe it was time for me to consider a more mature range of clothing when dressing. Perhaps tops with expanding waistlines were in fashion. I didn't own any white slacks, but I did have a white linen shirt which was now too tight around my exploding stomach. I had a light wrap I could have draped around my shoulders to create a carefree sort of feel like the grey haired menopause model, but I was so damn hot; I would have arrived at the doctors drenched in sweat. I had a few grey hairs coming through, especially around my forehead. Maybe with a bit more focus and work, I could actually pull off that carefree menopause woman's look!

Ok, so what to wear? Nothing fitted and at best, I could wear the white shirt that was too tight and that was it, but I would possibly have been arrested had I gone down that road. After rummaging around for a while, I found a maxi dress that would have to suffice but even that was tight. Once again, I felt I had absolutely no control over my body. I took myself and my stomach off to the doctor.

After an examination and a blood test to check hormone levels, the doctor confirmed that I was experiencing menopause. I had thought that menopause was reserved for really mature women but after a quick recount of how many birthdays I had celebrated, I realised that I was in fact one of those mature women.

Ageing is so strange. In your mind, you feel exactly the same as you did when you were really young. However the years lived have gifted you with this incredible wisdom, which is an unshakeable knowing and confidence that we are rewarded with. The passage of time, although sometimes challenging, is rich with blessings if we choose to acknowledge them. With our thoughts and experiences, we can pick and choose who we want to share our stories with, or our thoughts can remain private if we want. The body that carries us through this incredible journey can change dramatically for some of us as we age. With physical ageing of the body, it is a little harder to disguise some of the effects of gravity.

The media tends to favour youth and physical beauty. We are continuously bombarded with aesthetically beautiful women who have been Photoshopped to the max on magazine covers. The media dictates to us the definition of beauty, which can cause low self-esteem and trigger all sorts of struggles for many women around the world. Wouldn't it be nice if the media celebrated and showered us with images of the many millions of women who embody beauty at any age, no matter what shape or size they are? Women who embody energy, spirit, good health, confidence and warmth without Photoshop; women who are comfortable in their own skin – we should be celebrating this kind of beautiful.

So here I was, faced with the news that I was experiencing *the change*. After I gathered my thoughts and accepted the inevitable, I had to choose how I was going to manage this next adventure with my body as after all, I am in the driver's seat. The roads and the terrain may be challenging, but I have become a pretty good driver really. To start with, I looked at all my symptoms and found a way to reduce the severity of them. I looked at my diet and introduced sage tea to assist me with hot flushes and fatigue. I visited a wonderful naturopath who put me on magnesium powder for a multitude of symptoms. The magnesium powder helped me to sleep better and gave me a feeling of wellbeing. I decided with my doctor that I would try to deal with menopause day by day naturally first and as I progressed further into it, we would face each challenge accordingly. I strongly recommend working with a doctor and a naturopath with menopause. Don't go it alone. We have so many options available to us now. It's finding what works for you as an individual, as we are all so different. One size definitely does not fit everyone. Search high and low to find treatments that will support your personal needs.

I have stepped up my walking daily to help with my exploding belly. The belly increases because our oestrogen levels drop and our body fat is redistributed from the hips, thighs, and buttocks to the abdomen. Who would have thought that so much of my behind would relocate to the front! I have had to really examine the quality and the quantity of what I eat. Even how often I eat has changed, and I am finding smaller meals more frequently keep my energy levels up. The fatigue initially was a huge issue, so these small refuelling stops really help.

I made the decision swiftly to really embrace this change. I have committed to making a clear visual picture in my mind on how I will look and feel during this next stage. I think we amplify so many challenges in our mind, so closing my eyes for a few minutes each day and seeing myself breezing through the changes keeps it all in perspective. A healthy diet, rest, exercise, meditation, practitioner's vitamins, to date these are my key treatments for my menopause. Committing to them fully is a great way to manage every aspect of our health regardless.

Although managing *the change* requires self-discipline, self-love and a damn good pair of spanx, I am pleased to say, attitude is everything when it comes to menopause. Maybe that image of the grey-haired woman in the white slacks, shirt and cardie wasn't so misleading after all. We develop real self-confidence and also a sense of freedom as we mature. Perhaps we should all revel in the fact that it's a privilege to be able to smell the roses and bask in the sunshine and if *the change* is my biggest challenge to date, then I am truly blessed.

"Turn your face toward the sun and
the shadows will fall behind you."
—Maori quote

Chapter Eight

When life throws you curves

I know what it feels like to be a size six and I know what it feels like to be a size sixteen. It doesn't matter what size you are, it is almost as if some of us have been hardwired to find fault with our bodies. Over the years, I have fought with my body, starved it, over fed it, over exercised it and under exercised it. It has taken me years to actually wave the white flag and surrender to my naturally curvaceous shape. It has been one heck of a journey to achieve balance and accept that I am naturally a more curvaceous woman. I think perhaps I may have been born into the wrong era. I would have been totally 'en vogue' during the Renaissance period. During this time, voluptuous bodies were considered absolutely beautiful. Looking maternal, fertile and nurturing was really favoured; I would have fitted in perfectly.

At each stage though, my self-esteem has stayed firmly intact and that is one thing that has been unshakeable regardless of my size or shape. My size has never defined me. The number on the scales has never reflected my personality or my integrity, as it cannot measure my worth as a person. Is it thin thighs and flat stomachs that change the world? Absolutely not! It is women who are proud, passionate, confident and self-assured that really make a difference.

We have an intense exercise track near our home. Every day people run, walk and climb this track in order to improve their fitness and health. One particular morning when I was driving to the clinic to consult on wellness and weight loss, I was sitting in my car at an intersection waiting for the traffic lights to change. I watched the endless stream of men and women race towards the track to tackle the climb. I noticed one woman on this day amongst the hundreds of people exercising as her energy and confidence really caught my attention. This woman was about to walk the track. She was dressed in shorts and a white t-shirt and looked quite tanned, curvaceous and full figured. What stood out about her was that she just radiated good health. She looked fit and totally healthy; she was bounding with energy and was extremely proud of her body. I have to say, as I waited for those lights to change, I couldn't stop staring at her. Even from a distance her energy impacted me. Her confidence from afar changed the way I consulted and it also changed the way I looked at my own body.

To date, many of my clients would set a goal to lose a kilo a week. Sometimes they would aim really high and try to lose two kilos in a week. When weigh-in day came, if they only lost half a kilo they would instantly drop their bundle. The disappointment of not smashing their goal overshone the fact that they had just made a massive improvement to their health with all the positive changes they had made. The devastation of not cracking that number on the scales was enough to send them spiralling out of control and quit the whole healthy eating program.

From that day forward, when I consulted with clients, instead of setting weight loss goals, we set positive change goals. We removed the scales to see how successful we could be if we shifted our focus. Instead of measuring our success with how many kilos we lost, we measured our success with recording the number of positive changes we made. From walking an extra ten minutes every day, to eating more greens, from skipping all alcohol, to stretching and meditating daily, from drinking more water, to enrolling into Pilates. These became life-changing achievements; we shifted our focus from losing weight to gaining good health. The commitment to change had to be for life, so we signed contracts of commitment to forever quit dieting and instead embrace healthy eating and healthy living as a lifestyle. Week by week, I saw these massive changes in my clients. At each consultation, when we removed the scales and shared these enormous daily positive actions and life-changing commitments, suddenly goals towards getting healthy were being smashed out of the park.

We applauded one another when we walked an extra kilometre daily. High-fives were given when we went from consuming one glass of water a day to eight a day consistently. Suddenly everyone seemed to walk taller. Energy levels changed when we quit that fight with the scales and made peace with our bodies. Instead of feeling deprived by dieting, everyone felt uplifted and rejuvenated from all the incredible healthy choices being made and healthy activities being undertaken. It was life-changing and liberating. No-one felt restricted and instead felt empowered by their choices.

Instead of criticising our shapes, our waistlines and focussing on our weaknesses, we embraced them and found ways to support and nourish our individual needs. Instead of fighting with our bodies, we acknowledged that each curve, each wrinkle, each scar made up the story of who we were as individuals. We realised that thrashing about trying to attain something that wasn't achievable for our shapes or our individual makeup was not going to move us forward. Instead, every time we made better choices, we empowered ourselves and jumped ahead.

Day by day, week by week, everyone was rewarded with good health. Naturally, those that needed to lose weight did so at their own pace. Blood pressure dropped, cholesterol was reduced, and clients got fitter and shed kilos without even thinking about it. Most importantly, we acknowledged that one size does not fit everyone, especially when it comes to diet and exercise. Each and every one involved in my clinic got completely in touch with their own body. They embraced their curves, their individual shapes and worked on nurturing and loving themselves with positive change that filled them up and didn't strip them bare.

At every session, each client committed to working with their body and not against their body. The following positive affirmation became our mantra: *I love and accept every curve, every fold and every part of my body.*

Making peace with our body ultimately lies in realising that it is not our body that needs to change, it is actually our mindset and choices that need to change. If we stop the judgements and the criticism and actually embrace a new perspective that empowers us to feel beautiful, healthy and confident, when we give ourselves permission to be ourselves completely and nourish our body with healthy food, exercise and self-love, we release our mind, body and spirit from struggling.

Love yourself enough to make peace with your body no matter what shape you are. Accept that the only way to stop the struggle is to really appreciate all your curves, all your folds and all of your individual, beautiful imperfections. Embrace and love your body. It's the most amazing thing you will own.

"It is health that is real wealth and not pieces of gold and silver."
—Mahatma Ghandi

Chapter Nine

I quit dieting

We are bombarded with dietary options nowadays: Diet pills, meal replacements, shakes, special tonics that detox our systems promising dramatic weight loss; we have an endless supply of fad diets available to us. Some of these options work in the short term, but more often than not, the weight and some returns once we surrender to the fact that many of these diets are not sustainable.

Even the word diet conjures up feelings of deprivation. I have done plenty of diets over the years and I have tried weight loss pills unsuccessfully. It is so exhausting. I remember a friend and I both decided to do the cabbage soup diet for the recommended seven day period once when we were both attending a gala event. It was a nightmare for me. I felt physically exhausted and by day three, just looking at that soup made me cranky and irritable. I felt mentally drained and internally depleted, bowl after bowl. My friend lost four kilos in her seven day soup stint; she was ecstatic but also exhausted. I lost one kilo doing the same diet; I was annoyed as well as fatigued. *What a waste of a week, I thought. One kilo was hardly worth the effort, especially as I gained back the one I lost plus two more over the weekend!*

My battle stopped when I really learnt about good nutrition and accepted that achieving a healthy body requires healthy food, exercise, water, balance and self-love. Rinse and repeat this process every day for life. It can't be just one day a week or when you have to squeeze into a dress before a big event, you have to be consistent. When I accepted that embracing healthy eating as a lifestyle choice seven days a week was far more fulfilling then going on a diet, it was empowering. When I finally accepted that there wasn't a magic diet pill or a shake available that would provide me with what healthy eating does, that too was liberating, not to mention sensible.

There are so many people who instinctively know this information. It is a given that they always have and always will eat healthy food. It is like they arrived into the world naturally enlightened on the joys of healthy eating. Then there are the rest of us! We seem to be attracted to all the wrong foods. I have noticed that if you have food allergies, you seem to have a tendency to want to eat what you are actually allergic to. I love bread and pasta, but it doesn't love me back. If you are attracted to the wrong kinds of food daily, it is vital to retrain your brain to get really excited when we see a healthy salad over a creamy cake. It takes a little work, but it can be done. When you feel bloated and exhausted from consuming too much bad food, really feel the emotions associated with this. Write down everything you have eaten and examine which foods would have contributed to this unsettling feeling. It is important to start working out what foods uplift you, energise you and support your body. It is even more important to acknowledge what foods have the opposite effect.

Accept that eating unhealthy fats, processed foods, sweets, carbonated drinks, chips, fatty takeaways, may give you an instant hit of gratification and a bit of a high, but once digested you will be rewarded with a food hangover, excess weight, bloating and fatigue. Add to that list possible health issues like high blood pressure, obesity and diabetes and really associate those unhealthy foods with the negative results that they carry for you. You must focus on the cause and then the effect. Acknowledge that unhealthy foods on a daily basis will sabotage your health and your body. There is nothing worse than feeling uncomfortable from food. That lack of self-control associated with eating too much of the wrong foods can be soul destroying.

We have to eat healthy foods daily and then totally immerse ourselves in the wonderful feelings that accompany nutritious, healthy eating. The rewards are endless. If you have been a die-hard junk food addict, quitting the bad food and choosing a healthy meal over an unhealthy meal is absolutely uplifting. Making the decision to eat something healthy is something to be proud of. We must focus on the positive outcomes and make a firm commitment to avoid those foods that drag us down.

If you have a beautiful home and you spend hours and hours a week ensuring that your house is in tip-top shape, you wouldn't dare destroy this investment by dumping rubbish inside of it because this is where you live. You keep it clean and you look after it, right? It is pride that motivates us to create a healthy living space. Your body really is the only place that you have to live, it is your temple, your home and you need to nourish and maintain it. Don't fill it with rubbish. Just because you can't see what is happening inside, doesn't mean that it is in tip-top condition. You wouldn't purposely walk into your lounge room and throw garbage all over the carpet would you? Why do some of us find it acceptable to fill our bodies full of garbage food? And weight may not be an issue for you, but just because you are slender doesn't automatically make you healthy.

It takes three weeks to break a habit, so if you have developed unhealthy eating habits, accept the fact that once you commit to quitting the unhealthy food, you may still have a few cravings that will test your willpower. So when you feel the urge to eat something bad, when that craving hits, the best way to handle it is to distract yourself. Instead of focussing intently on how badly you want that unhealthy treat, refocus. Go for a walk, phone a friend, hang out the washing, meditate, take a shower or just simply remind yourself that the rewards for reaching for a healthy snack will far outweigh the obvious. A craving is a little like a wave, it starts rolling in, gets stronger, peaks and then it gently rolls away. Train yourself to ride the craving wave out and allow yourself at least ten or fifteen minutes for the urge to pass.

I no longer diet. Instead I eat healthy food when I am hungry and I mean fresh fruit, fresh vegetables, lean protein, dairy, some grains, herbs and I drink lots of water. I try not to overeat, as I hate that feeling of being so full that it hurts. I also hate that feeling of disappointment associated with continued mindless eating.

Some people will never struggle with food issues, and then there are many people that will. Comfort eating, mindless eating, over eating, whatever we want to label it, we all have the ability to over indulge, but we all also have the ability to choose. We can choose to quit dieting and embrace healthy eating and we can choose to focus on good health and wellness daily.

The first step comes with loving yourself enough to fill your body with soul food and by soul food, I mean food that energises us, uplifts us and invigorates us. Soul food is good for our soul and our bodies respond by showering us with good health, wellness and balance. Think attainable, sustainable and long term. Think healthy eating for life.

"Food is medicine, and the right kind of relationship with food can make a positive impact on your health."
—Hayley Hobson

Chapter Ten

Loving you is easy because you are beautiful

It is absolutely vital to love, nurture and respect yourself and your body. It doesn't matter what your battle is, negative self-talk does not bring you any closer to achieving your goals. More often than not when having coffee with friends, you can guarantee that the conversation will always include some reference to bloating, losing weight, messy hair, being on a diet and of course there is always the wrinkles forming to have a chat about. A recent survey has suggested that women have an average of thirteen negative things to say about themselves every day. Two-thirds of women surveyed in the United States reported that their weight and shape negatively impacts their lives on a daily basis. It is also reported that just two per cent of women chose the word 'beautiful' to describe themselves. Body issues, appearance issues and low self-esteem exist within all age groups. It is devastating to think that so many women wake up in the morning and their mood, their outlook and even their energy levels are determined by their bathroom scales or how they perceive themselves when they look in the mirror.

If you are someone who constantly criticises yourself, whether it be your body, your weight, your hair, your performance, or your appearance, don't you think it is high time you stopped the negative self-talk? You wouldn't openly criticise someone else to their face, would you? You wouldn't speak to someone you love so brutally, would you? Then why do it to yourself? Are you paying attention to your inner dialogue as well as how you express yourself verbally? Constantly berating yourself is soul destroying; it won't bring you peace.

Over the years, I have witnessed firsthand clients beating up on themselves. They verbally abuse themselves for being too fat, for not reaching a weight loss goal and for even giving in to temptation and indulging in a piece of cake. I have heard how hopeless they are at so many things, how stupid they are and even how their siblings are smarter and better looking than them! Seriously, I have heard a lot of negative self-talk from clients. It is actually so normal for them to criticise themselves that they don't even realise they are doing it. I will normally listen for a few minutes and then I will bring their destructive self-criticism to their attention and ask them to stop and really pay attention to how they are speaking about themselves. Whether it is internal dialogue or verbal dialogue, I ask them to listen to themselves slowly chipping away at their self-esteem.

I will normally ask a client to stop and close their eyes, then ask them to visualise themselves as a three year old child who is visibly upset. I will ask them to see themselves as adults standing in front of this small upset child. I will then ask them how they feel and what do they want to do for this little person. It is at this point that they realise that they want to nurture and comfort this small child and instinctively want to soothe and wipe away those tears. It is obvious that they have a desperate need to gather this child up to protect and love it. Once they have acknowledged this feeling, I ask them to open their eyes and look directly at themselves in the mirror.

It is astounding the powerful effect that this simple visualisation exercise has on people. They see themselves differently and acknowledge that their inner child deserves love, nurturing and encouragement. It does not deserve to be criticised. You know making peace with our bodies ultimately lies in realising that it is actually not our bodies that need changing, it is our actual mindset that needs adjusting. If we stop the judgements, the criticisms, the comparisons and quit the negative self-talk, we are taking a giant step forward in celebrating ourselves. When we make the decision to change the way we view our bodies and how we speak about our bodies, we are giving ourselves permission to be whole.

What do we gain by being critical, preoccupied and dissatisfied with our bodies? The answer is absolutely nothing! Make the decision to flat out refuse to speak badly about yourself from this moment on. If you consistently obsess about what is wrong with you, it is impossible to acknowledge what is right with you. Changing how you talk to yourself is another habit you will need to either break or create. Your goal is to make positive self-talk second nature. Honour yourself and acknowledge that you are beautiful. Respect your purpose, your mind, your body and remind yourself daily of just how incredible you really are.

Do you have daughters, sons, nieces, nephews, grand-children? Our children really pick up on their parents' and role models' anxieties. They learn from us. If we engage in negative language about our bodies and how we look in front of our children, what kind of message are we sending them? What you say, how you act, how you express yourself in front of your children, it matters.

If you openly speak negatively about yourself in front of your children, remember, your children are listening. You are shaping and influencing their future and your words matter.

A healthy body does not always equate to a healthy body image and our kids will pick up on our constant quests to be thinner or whatever it is we are trying to achieve. The media certainly has played its part in sending us messages about what women should look like. The more images we are presented with on what is considered beautiful, the more we believe we should strive to achieve that look, even though for many of us it is genetically impossible. So many women are striving to achieve standards that are often physically impossible for them.

Beauty isn't perfect. Nobody is perfect. Life isn't perfect. Self-acceptance, self-love, gratitude, and nourishing our bodies, our minds and our spirits with nutritious food, positive self-talk and practices that allow us to shine, now that's healthy! Be gentle with yourself; you are a limited edition. There is no-one else like you, so celebrate every part of you from the top of your head to the tip of your toes and repeat after me, *I completely love and accept myself.*

"You have been criticising yourself for years and it hasn't worked. Try approving of yourself and see what happens."

—Louise Hay

Chapter Eleven

Because you are worth it

When we arrive in this world, we are born with a full tank of self-esteem. Little by little over time, this tank gets depleted. Expectations that can't be met, bullying behaviour from others, negative environments, these are all tank drainers. Certain life challenges can deplete our self-esteem more than others and we are all uniquely different when it comes to how we manage and conserve our tank.

Some of us have the great privilege of being born into families that naturally keep their self-esteem tanks full constantly and understand the value of this precious commodity. Then there are others who are born into environments where there are little resources available to refuel. Other people around who are also low on self-esteem will readily tap into other people's tanks to top up their low self-esteem levels.

Imagine each and every one of us is born with an inbuilt self-esteem tank. It is just like the fuel tank in your car except the gauge to this self-esteem tank is located and visible on your forehead. Just like the fuel gauge in your car, it consists of two parts, the sensing unit and the indicator. The sensing unit tracks just how much self-esteem you have on a daily basis, meanwhile, the indicator keeps a visible record for you so that you can monitor whether your tank is full or empty. When you are confident, full of self-love and value yourself, the indicator needle points to 'F'. You know you can change the whole world when you have a full tank of self- esteem, it is powerful, energetic, contagious and the most valuable form of energy to possess. When this tank is empty, the gauge points to 'E' indicating an empty tank. When your self-esteem tank is empty, you have no energy, you are easily taken advantage of, you feel drained and just like a car, you may require someone to give you a push to keep you moving forward. The problem we all face as humans is that we actually do not have that visible gauge to rely on. Many people realise that they are low on self-esteem as they can feel it draining away, but they don't stop to fill up their tank often enough. They just keep pushing to get through on low resources and then one day they realise when they are *all out* just how precious self-esteem is.

We simply cannot rely on other people to keep our self-esteem tanks topped up. We are personally responsible for managing our health, our lives and our self-worth. True self-worth comes from deep within. Acknowledging that our health is important, our contribution to the world is important, our role as mothers, grandmothers, daughters, granddaughters, sisters, these are all vital. We must love ourselves enough to accept that each day as we walk this earth, we have the opportunity to really shine. We individually have qualities that we can share with the world. Maybe you are a mum, teacher, nurse, artist, a great listener, wonderful friend, a world leader even, whatever it is that you do, you make a difference. You are a valued and treasured part of this community we call the world. Your qualities, your beautiful contributions daily whether they are big or small, are not defined by your weight, your shape or how you look. They are defined by your heart. Your self-esteem is shaped by your thoughts, your actions, your contributions and the value you place on all of your personal achievements and attributes.

It is our birthright to have a healthy amount of self-worth. Although it is wonderful to be acknowledged and recognised for all that we do by others, it really is important to understand that it is actually our own responsibility to see that we are worthy, valuable and incredibly special. If you hold other people in high esteem for their qualities, their achievements, their contributions, it is important to accept that we are absolutely worthy of our own love and affection and recognition.

If you love someone, you naturally treat them with respect. It is vital that you treat yourself the same way. Building self-esteem and filling up your own tank requires acknowledging that we require nurturing. We must nurture ourselves physically, emotionally, spiritually and mentally; the benefits we get when we do this are enormous. Self-care provides the fuel we need to fill up our self-esteem tanks. Self-care and making better choices with all areas of your health and your life is empowering. When we take care of ourselves, we show our children, our friends and our loved ones an example of positive self-esteem. If we respect our bodies and make healthy choices every day in regard to food and exercise, we will absolutely be rewarded with good health, a healthy body, increased energy and a full tank of self-esteem.

If we do just a few things regularly to renew our energy and revitalise our spirit, like witness a sunrise or sunset, hug our loved ones, laugh with our friends, walk on the beach, this will improve our wellbeing and add sparkle to the soul as well as fuel to the tank. If we say no to perfectionism, criticism, procrastination, comparisons and we are mindful of how we invest our precious energy daily, we will keep our self-esteem up. If we express our needs, wants, values and boundaries clearly and confidently, this will keep self-esteem levels well and truly overflowing. The more energy you invest in yourself, the more self-esteem will be deposited into your tank. We must keep topping our tanks up daily. Refuelling our self-esteem tank is as important as cleaning our teeth! Dig down deep and realise just how precious you are. Believing that you are worthy of your own love, respect, affection and recognition, starts at the source of this tank. Keeping it well fuelled is a sign that you are sincerely grateful for all that you have and for all that you are. You know the way you treat yourself really does set the standard for how others treat you and how the world sees you. Make peace with yourself today. You are good enough, great enough, and gorgeous enough. Hold yourself in high esteem!

"Self-worth comes from one thing. Thinking that you are worthy."
—Dr Wayne Dyer

Chapter Twelve

The perfect body

I am sorry to inform you, there is absolutely no such thing as a perfect body. We come in all shapes and sizes and each one of us will see different aspects of beauty in one another. A tall slim woman can be seen as perfect by one person and far too thin by another. A curvaceous woman can be seen as womanly, sexy and feminine by one person and overweight by another. Beauty absolutely is in the eye of the beholder. We cannot select one body type and then label it as perfect. Striving to have a healthy body will bring far greater results than striving to have a perfect body.

When you think about your body, do you ever focus on the parts that you love? Or do you constantly prioritise, focussing on the parts that bug you? I challenge you to really get to know your body. Stand in front of a mirror and seriously examine it; look at every detail. Acknowledge every curve, every fold, every crease and every single part of it.

Initially, when we strip ourselves bare and really look underneath our clothes, it can be a little overwhelming, even intimidating. Do not pay attention to what your mind is saying. Shut down the thoughts that are criticising and finding fault and resist the urge to look at yourself negatively. Instead, focus intensely on the parts of your body you love. It may be your curvaceous hips, it may be your elegant neck, your beautiful calves, your shapely legs, your beautiful face, your gorgeous hair and your stunning eyes. Recognise, acknowledge and accept that your body is beautiful, you are beautiful. Quite frankly, you are a work of art; a masterpiece! Stand tall and accentuate all of your glorious features. Look at yourself, I mean really look at every inch of you. Keep doing this exercise every day, until your mind finally acknowledges that your body is beautiful.

Your body and your face tell your life story. Your scars reflect your battles and fights. For some women, these scars symbolise survival. Your lines and wrinkles are imprints of a life truly lived and a symbol of wisdom, wisdom that only comes with age. Your shape is uniquely you. In a completely image obsessed society, we should be standing proud and loving our perfect imperfections. Instead of accepting what we are being told is 'perfect', question it. When you look in the mirror and get to know your body, make sure you think about whose beauty ideal it is that you are comparing yourself to. Quite frankly, you are in charge of this, no-one else.

Your beauty, your body's beauty is not determined by your weight or your shape. You simply shine when you choose to not be dictated to or defined by the commercial ideals of what some consider perfection. Every BODY is beautiful; we all embody beauty. When you feel free and comfortable in your own skin, when you completely respect the journey your body has taken you on, when you accept yourself completely, you are beautiful. When you meet someone who lights up a room, has a compassionate heart, laughs with gusto and carries themselves through life confidently, we don't include their size or shape in this list of attributes. Self-acceptance of our imperfections is truly beautiful. Expressing gratitude for all your body does for you will help you to realise how amazingly beautiful your body is right now. Think of all the wonderful things you experience through your body. The list of joyous things your body can do for you is only limited by the boundaries you set for it.

I spent some years after my son was born on a quest to try and create the perfect body for myself. I had battled glandular fever and lost a lot of weight. At first, I really loved being able to fit into clothes that had not been an option for me for some years. In order to maintain this new body, I would walk for an hour in the morning, go to the gym for an hour during the day and then try and do another walk at night. The old addictive gene and the endorphins kicking in from all the exercise kept me committed to working towards the illusive perfect shape. I never found that perfect shape because I never acknowledged just how perfect my body was to begin with. It felt like I was actually fighting against my body instead of supporting my body as my exercise regime wasn't balanced. My thinness did not suit me because it was not a comfortable fit for the real me. It was exhausting trying to support a shape that my body struggled to maintain.

After a few years of battling with a gruelling exercise regime, I knew if I stopped to breathe, I would just burst! Burst out of my seams so to speak and that seemed crazy to have spent so much time creating something that I could not maintain. I had to really change my focus from what I could do, rather than what I couldn't do and to what I did have, instead of what I didn't have! I can work out for hours a day, or an hour a day and I will never achieve that stereotyped perfection.

I am not a runner, I am a walker. I would rather swim and splash around in the sea than do laps in an Olympic chlorinated pool. I would rather walk in the rainforest than sweat it out in the gym. I would rather do Zumba with my friends than do an aerobics class. I now choose to exercise in a way that makes me feel joyous and exhilarated. Some people prefer hard core training, marathon running, and mountain climbing; it's all about finding what strengthens your body and makes you feel amazing. There is no right or wrong. It is finding what makes you feel strong personally.

Real body confidence only comes when we embrace the skin we are in. Let's not waste any more time on obsessing about being perfect, instead invest in achieving a healthy body. Self-awareness, self-love and real acceptance of your body will bring you peace. Let's all celebrate our uniqueness. Do not be dictated to about what society sees as perfect, fashionable, on trend or even beautiful. Instead accept and love every inch of you. We have an opportunity as women to join together and make a difference. Let's celebrate beauty in all its forms.

"The day she let go of the things that were weighing her down, was the day she began to shine her brightest."

—Katrina Mayer

Chapter Thirteen

Listen to your body

Your body is constantly communicating with you. Are you actually paying attention? Are you listening to it or are you ignoring it? When you really listen to the signs and symptoms your body is giving you, whether it be hunger, pain or fatigue, you are actually developing an understanding of what it needs and when it needs it. If you were to really stop and pay more attention to these signs and signals and then look at your lifestyle choices, you can begin to work out how to manage your personal wellness.

More often than not, we get up each morning and we just go through the motions of our daily rituals and routines. You may be struggling with all sorts of niggling issues, and yet we just somehow push through, often ignoring these signs that are signalling us to take action. Soldiering on is certainly admirable, but unless you look at the root of the problem and acknowledge it and change it, it is going to continue.

Good health and wellness doesn't need to be complicated. Getting in touch with your body along with addressing lifestyle problems, will contribute to managing your health and it can improve your entire life. If you spend most of your days on Google searching for the miracle treatment for anti-ageing and the secret to weight loss, your time would be far better spent listening to your own body. You can actually just trust your body to keep you well informed of what is right for it and what is definitely wrong for it.

I am not sure why so many of us ignore the crucial messages our bodies are sending us. Some of us Band-Aid health issues because we don't have enough time to address them. Being time poor or maybe even scared to face the challenge is not a good enough reason to ignore your wellness as often simple lifestyle changes is all it takes to avoid major fallout. Don't ignore the signs from your body telling you that it is unhappy. If a health issue gets so out of control and is not managed, the results can be devastating not only for you but also for your loved ones. Take notice and listen to your body. Don't ignore pain, anxiety, stress, fatigue or any niggling problem no matter how small it is. This is your body signalling you to pay attention. It is simple nowadays to go and get a check-up from a healthcare practitioner.

Every single cell in your body reacts to negative emotions, injury, unhealthy relationships, unhealthy food, negative self-talk, too much alcohol, stress, allergens, not enough sunshine and too much darkness. Some of these cells really shake us up to ensure we are aware that we are ticking them off! You can be well and truly assured that your body will respond if you are not putting in the energy to nourish and support it. If we stop ignoring all the signs and start to recognise them as warnings, we can then take positive action.

If you are thirsty, your body is signalling you that you are dehydrated or maybe even hungry as thirst and hunger can be confused. If you are fatigued constantly, perhaps your diet really needs an overhaul or maybe you are not moving enough. There could even be an underlying issue that needs addressing associated with the tiredness; there are many reasons for fatigue. Pain is a sign of inflammation, so ignoring any kind of pain is not advisable. Stress and anxiety can be a symptom of absolute overload and we have so much available to us now to help manage these conditions, so reach out and get help.

Whatever the issue, your body is sending you messages. Signs and signals are different for everybody. We are all wired differently so what is acceptable for you may not be acceptable for someone else. It's important to learn to interpret your body's individual messages. You are unique.

The choices you make today with regards to your health influence your future health. There is no better time than right now to take personal responsibility for your body. Getting in touch with your body and learning to listen to it is one of the best ways to actually make peace with it. Combine this with healthy lifestyle changes and your body will really reward you with energy and good health.

Often just getting back to the basics and taking a holistic, simple approach to wellness can bring huge benefits. Be gentle with yourself and love yourself enough to make your wellness a priority. Your body is constantly providing you with information. Are you listening? Always pay attention to your body; it is smarter than you think.

"If you listen to your body when it whispers,
you will never have to listen to it scream."
—author unknown

Chapter Fourteen

Peace treaty

It is not often we stop to really appreciate how amazing our bodies are. Your body is resilient; it is miraculous how it can heal after an injury or an illness. It brings us joy, pleasure and yes, pain. It's amazing how it responds when we really look after it and reconnect with it. When I first began my job as a wellness specialist, I would often ask my clients to write a personal letter to their body. Writing yourself a letter is a great way to look at how you have treated or mistreated your body over the years. It is a beautiful way to wave the white flag and make peace. I wrote myself a letter of apology over seven years ago, and this formal peace treaty completely changed my relationship with my body. It allowed me to acknowledge my past mistakes and this simple act gave me an opportunity to formally take ownership of my actions and choices. It was one of the very first steps in making peace. I would like to share my letter with you.

Dear Body,

I want to start by apologising. We have had a real love-hate relationship for such a long time now. I apologise for those early years of keeping you up all night long, drinking and dancing and then consuming bad food to soothe the hangover. I don't know what I was thinking. Filling you with cocktails, cigarette smoke and bad food must have been exhausting for you. I was only focussed on enjoying myself for all the wrong reasons.

I apologise for torturing you to the point of exhaustion because I wanted to get rid of your gorgeous curves. I even pushed you when you were injured to keep going. I didn't let up and I showed no mercy. I am sorry for depriving you of food in an effort to be skinny. I am just as sorry that I over fed you with foods that you were clearly allergic to. I should have listened when you were showing me that you were hurting.

I apologise for criticising you, even calling you fat. Loving you one day and then insulting you the next must have been confusing. I apologise for completely ignoring you, verbally abusing you and treating you with such disregard.

I promise from this day forward to never disrespect you again. You have continuously given me messages. I will listen, respect and appreciate you from now on. I have so much planned for the future; I need you to carry me through a whole lifetime.

I promise to work with you, not against you. Thank you for allowing me the greatest gift of bringing my beautiful *son into this world. Thank you for allowing me to walk, run, dance and swim. Thank you for the privilege of experiencing touch, sight, taste, excitement, love, hugs – privileges many people don't have.*

Thank you for always repairing and healing, allowing me to get back up, again privileges many people are denied. I love and respect every inch, every curve, and every fold of you.

I am grateful for every feeling and emotion you bring me. Thank you, and I completely love and accept you – just the way you are.

Jo

I strongly recommend that every woman write a letter to their body. It is a beautiful way to make peace and begin a new relationship with yourself. Take the time to write and sign a peace treaty with your body today, make friends, fall in love and create a loving relationship with you. Take the first step today in reconnecting, repairing and rejuvenating one of the most important relationships of your life.

"No matter how hard the past, you can always begin again."
—Buddha

Chapter Fifteen

Brand new day

There is no denying it; I have really had a troubled relationship with my body. For many years, we have been enemies. I have experienced so many stages and changes with my body and have had highs and extreme lows. I know women in their fifties who basically have retained the same shape since high school and have done it with such ease. I however have gone up, down and sideways with my body; finding that balance has taken me a long time. Balance is the key and it is an integral part of having a peaceful relationship with the body. Doing the opposite of what your body is signalling you to do will create all sorts of problems.

Although my self-confidence has always been in abundance, I have done my fair share of criticising my body in private. Being at war with oneself is exhausting, debilitating and destructive. It wasn't until I absolutely addressed every negative lifestyle choice, educated myself on healthy eating, quit dieting, quit criticising and started to really respect my body that I began to heal and find relief.

I also accepted that wellness encompasses so much more than just diet and exercise. The mind and the spirit also require nurturing. Feeding these areas with nourishing thoughts, peaceful, calming practices and complete respect have changed my life. Don't get me wrong, I embody that same wild, young free-spirited woman now in my fifties. She is still very much there, but I have tamed her ways and really value my health as good health is absolutely priceless. The decisions I make on a daily basis now support wellness. When you finally make peace with your body and acknowledge how wonderful it is to feel clear, energetic and healthy, it is exhilarating. You cannot help but fall in love with your body and its brilliance.

It takes a conscious decision from deep within to let go of what has been weighing you down. In order to move forward and release yourself from the awful internal struggle with body image, we must first address unhealthy lifestyle habits.

In order to change our lives we must change the way we look at ourselves and this can be confronting. Taking responsibility for the negative things we do can be hard work, but if we want to move forward we absolutely must stop, address and be accountable for our choices. These choices are in relation to food, exercise and self-talk. Understand that it can be one step forward and two steps back on this journey to make peace. If we have been conditioned to view ourselves negatively, we can easily slip back into our old habits without even realising. Once you have made that decision to free yourself from struggling, there is no going back. Those old thoughts and habits may creep back in from time to time, but you have the power to actually control this. You must pay careful attention to your thoughts. Initially, this can be challenging, but it gets easier and easier the more you become aware of what you are focussing on. Every brand new day presents you with the opportunity to choose. You can choose to love yourself more than unhealthy food. You can choose to move more. You can choose to speak to yourself with love. You can choose to make your own rules when it comes to your life instead of following someone else's. You can choose to love and accept yourself completely.

We have always been encouraged to put our best foot forward when we go out into the world and this is a great way to impress the masses. I say, put your best foot forward every day, but do it for you first. It is a far better idea to impress yourself completely. Being impressed with yourself is a vital step towards making peace. Get impressed when you choose healthy food over unhealthy food; get impressed when you take the stairs instead of the elevator; get impressed with all of your attributes. Make the most of them and don't do it for anyone else but you. Your opinion of yourself is far more valuable than anyone else's.

Throughout my own personal battles, I have remained committed to not allowing my weight, my shape or my size determine my self-worth. Do not let the number on the scales or the fact that you can fit into a certain size define you.

As women, we are powerful, we are beautiful, we are resilient, we are strong, we are gentle, we are determined, we are leaders, we are mothers, we are daughters, we are sisters, we change lives and we change the world. It is not our shape or size that drives us to achieve, it is our minds and our hearts. If you are wasting your life fighting with your body, your appearance and your self-esteem, just imagine what you could achieve and how you would feel if you put just as much energy into focussing on how beautiful you are right now.

I wrote this book to remind every woman in the world that when you believe in yourself, when you love yourself, when you stop fighting and make peace with whatever your struggle is, your whole life will change. Celebrate how incredibly spectacular you are and begin a brand new relationship with your body. The most important relationship you will ever have is the relationship that you have with yourself. Today is a brand new day and a perfect day to fall in love with you.

"Stop trying to fix yourself. You are not broken.
You are perfectly imperfect and powerful beyond measure."
—Steve Maraboli

PART TWO

Your Guide to Making Peace

Making peace, achieving balance and learning to love yourself requires daily commitment. Your wellbeing is important, so in order to feel really vibrant, understand that every day you must take the necessary steps to nourish, heal and uplift your body, mind and spirit. Eating healthy food, exercising, positive self-talk and self-nurturing. These acts have to become a part of your daily routine. There is no beauty tonic or magic pill that will heal and nourish you as well as self-love and self-care.

STEP ONE: ACKNOWLEDGING LIFESTYLE CHOICES

The first step in making peace with your body begins with acknowledging all of the unhealthy decisions we have made to date. We may have been conditioned to make unhealthy choices in regards to lifestyle, food, exercise and even self-talk, but in order to change we have to take ownership of how we treat ourselves. You cannot move forward without recognising what it is that we do on a daily basis that contributes to all the self-angst. Begin by asking yourself the following ten questions. Write down an honest answer to each one.

1:   Does my current diet support a healthy body?

2:   Do I consume more unhealthy food than healthy food? If the answer is yes, why?

3: Do I understand what healthy eating is?

4: Do I incorporate regular exercise into my week? If the answer is no, why not?

5: Have I really found an exercise regime that I enjoy? If the answer is no, why not?

6: How do I generally feel about myself?

7: Do I constantly criticise myself, my appearance and my body? If the answer is yes, why?

8: Do I continuously start diets, exercise plans, only to return to my unhealthy habits after a few days? If the answer is yes, why?

9: Do I take responsibility for my own wellness? If the answer is no, why not?

10: Am I tired of fighting with my body and my negative thinking on a daily basis?

Write down an honest answer to each question.
The answers may be as simple as –

• I don't have time to eat healthy food.

• I don't have time to exercise.

- I am used to criticising myself.

- I have no willpower.

- I don't know where to start.

- I am confused.

- I am too tired.

By writing down an honest response to each question, you will soon realise what areas require your urgent attention. Once you have examined and accepted what needs changing, create a lifestyle plan immediately that you can easily follow daily. It doesn't need to be complicated, it just needs to be clear, concise and realistic. It needs to have achievable strategies that you can implement every day. Keeping it simple is less overwhelming when it comes to change. It is important to have your plan in front of you and sight it as often as you can throughout your day, so that each change becomes second nature.

You may find that your lifestyle plan will need adjusting month by month. As you start to feel healthier and more positive, you may be able to introduce more activities that will promote a more illuminated you. When you write your lifestyle plan, write it in a loving way and remind yourself minute by minute why you deserve self-care.

Example of a Basic Lifestyle Plan:

6:00am

Wake up, stretch and breathe deeply for ten minutes.

I will walk briskly for twenty minutes.

I deserve to feel relaxed and energised. This is a positive way to start my day and I am setting the precedent for a productive, wonderful day.

I will take a few minutes to give thanks for all that is wonderful in my life.

6:30am

Consume a healthy breakfast — Herbal tea, fresh fruit and yoghurt.

I will kick start my metabolism with beautiful fresh food that is full of nutritious value. This food will fuel me and energise me and my body deserves to be nourished.

7:00am

I will shower and prepare for my day. I will spend this next thirty minutes pampering myself. I deserve to feel amazing and I will take the time to make myself feel beautiful. I will do this for me and only me. I will focus on all of my positive attributes in this next thirty minutes.

7:30am — 8:30am

I will get organised for the day ahead. I will use this time to prepare for a wonderful day and also remind myself of the following commitments I have made to myself:

TODAY — There will be absolutely no negative self-talk. I will say NO to perfectionism, gossip, criticism and negative thinking. I will commit to making healthy choices with food. I will do the best I can and every action I take will support my healthy lifestyle goals. I will drink more water.

8:30am — Work

I will commit to only speaking positively about myself and my work this morning. I will keep an optimistic outlook.

12:30 — Lunch

I will enjoy my beautifully prepared healthy lunch.

I will take five minutes to step outside and breathe deeply before I go back to work. This will clear my head and I deserve to recharge. Drink water.

1:00pm — Work

I will commit to only speaking positively about myself and my work this afternoon. I will keep an optimistic outlook.

5:30pm — 6:00pm — Swimming

I will swim for thirty minutes. It will relax me and help me to unwind after a productive day.

6:30pm

I will cook a nutritious beautiful dinner and also prepare lunch for work tomorrow to save time. I will prepare a meal that supports good health.

8:30pm

Time to shower and pamper my body. I will prepare for a beautiful night's sleep. My body needs rest and I will wake up refreshed. I will only focus on all of my positive achievements from today before I sleep and reflect on how blessed I am.

9:00pm

Herbal tea time and a little reading of my favourite book. I deserve this downtime.

My mind, body and spirit needs to slow down and recharge.

9:30pm — 10:00pm

I will take the time to reflect on what a fantastic day it has been. I will acknowledge all of my wonderful achievements and be grateful for this day. I will remind myself that I deserve my own love and affection and I will also meditate for ten minutes prior to sleeping.

10:00pm — Sleep well.

Now, this lifestyle plan is just a guideline or an example of how you can begin to create yours. Your days may be pretty hectic, but you absolutely must schedule the time in for taking breaks, eating healthily, getting fresh air, recharging and taking stock of where your thoughts are going. Your plan is your blue print. Its purpose is to keep you grounded and on track and to remind you that your wellness is your most valuable asset.

If you continuously say you are too busy or do not have the time to eat properly or even exercise, you are basically reinforcing the fact that you think that you are not worth the effort. Finding time is all about prioritising. Prioritising your goals in regards to wellness is paramount.

Although it seems simple enough to write a lifestyle plan, it is absolutely one of the most important steps in creating change. It will assist you to achieve your goals and keep you on track. Successful businesses are created by following business plans. Beautiful buildings are built based on written and drawn architectural plans. A lifestyle plan will keep you on track day by day, hour by hour and for those of you that have been winging it daily with little success, a lifestyle plan will keep you accountable.

Firmly commit to your lifestyle plan. As soon as each step becomes routine, revamp your plan. When it is second nature, add more goals and more positive activities to your day. Remember that consistent healthy actions practised daily become habits and then those habits become an automatic part of our thought process. Your lifestyle plan is a valuable tool and a wonderful first step in turning your world around.

STEP TWO: SELF TALK

Words have so much power. Every emotion we experience can be communicated through words. Love, joy, kindness, sympathy, happiness, pleasure, excitement, appreciation and gratitude are all emotions that can be explained and shared in words. Powerful, positive, beautiful words can heal and uplift, and when spoken from the heart, your words have the ability to change lives.

We have continuous mind chatter, consisting of words both positive and negative, continuously live streaming from the second we wake until we fall asleep. As vital as it is to pay attention to how we speak and communicate with others, it is even more important to pay attention to the internal dialogue we have with ourselves. Often we become programmed to continuously run negative thoughts, especially about our bodies.

Negative self-talk and self-criticism is destructive; it will drain your self-esteem. Our minds are paying careful attention to those thoughts we are having. Negative thoughts will impact our health, our quality of life and every part of our demeanour. Negative self-talk will completely sabotage every attempt you make to achieve peace.

How often do you think or verbalise the following thoughts?

- I am so tired

- I look tired

- I am fat

- I am stupid

- I wish I looked like (fill in the blank)

- I hate my (fill in the blank)

Do you do it occasionally? Do you do it often? Do you do it every time you look in the mirror? Have you ever acknowledged just how often you do this? I want you to spend the next twenty-four hours paying careful attention to your thoughts. What are you focussing on? How do you speak about yourself?

Let's consider the following exercise to understand how negative thoughts affect our energy and how we feel. Have you ever listened to a really sad song? When you listen to a sad song and focus on the words, your energy is instantly affected. You slow down, you feel depressed and given the right environment, you can even be brought to tears. Play that sad song long enough, over and over again and you will be reduced physically and mentally.

Now, stop and think. Have you ever listened to a really happy, upbeat, positive song? Think along the lines of *Happy* by Pharrell Williams. When we listen to a tune that is light, fun and positively charged, our bodies and our minds respond accordingly. We feel optimistic, brighter and we are uplifted, our mood and energy changes. What track are you running internally? Are the lyrics negative and destructive or are they positive and upbeat? Do you need to transform your internal vocabulary about yourself? If your biggest enemy is you, it is time to call a truce.

Positive self-talk is a vital step in making peace with your body. It is a phenomenal strategy for change. Some of the greatest athletes in the world use positive self-talk to help them achieve their biggest goals. The thing is, you actually don't need to be a gold medallist to use this strategy, anyone can do it. Just like a radio station, you can change the channel if you are sick to death of listening to that same old exhausting soundtrack.

Let's look at the initial steps you need to take in order to change self-talk from negative to positive. Start paying attention to your self-talk. More often than not, it is so routine to speak negatively about yourself; you are completely unaware of how frequently you do it. Really listen to how often you speak negatively about yourself or to yourself. For the next twenty-four hours, just keep a little tally of how often it happens. This will help you to realise firstly, that you are doing it, secondly, how often you are doing it and it will also begin the necessary process of interrupting this destructive habit. As you pay more attention to these thoughts, start asking yourself questions.

- Would I speak to my best friend like this?

- Would I speak to someone I loved like this?

- Am I being realistic or am I just being cruel?

- Can I change the situation?

- Am I actively taking positive steps towards feeling better?

- What resulted from saying something so negative to myself?

Make a commitment to quit the negative self-talk. Just like any toxic bad habit, decide to stop. It can take a little time, it can require perseverance, attention and strength to quit completely, as for many it has become so deeply ingrained, it is second nature. Understand that you will need to keep interrupting negative self-talk every time you realise you are doing it to stop it altogether. Becoming aware of this behaviour is the key to quitting.

Take the necessary steps to clean up your vocabulary. Remove negative descriptive words like fat, ugly, unhappy, tired, fed up; there is an endless supply of them, and replace them with words that are positive.

You know how uplifting it is when someone pays you a genuine compliment. Well, don't wait for that to happen. Be your own best friend and tell yourself constantly how amazing you are. Don't focus on what bugs you, focus solely on what you love about yourself. At every opportunity talk about yourself positively. If someone enquires about your wellbeing, don't use negative descriptive words to respond. For example, if someone says, 'How are you going?' tell them you are feeling fantastic! Get into the healthy habit of uplifting yourself through positive language.

Our self-talk fuels our health, our wellbeing and our self-esteem. Commit to cleaning up the dirty words. Always speak to yourself lovingly. Your words can make or break you.

STEP THREE: ACKNOWLEDGING YOUR BEAUTY

We can waste so much energy picking, criticising and finding fault with our bodies; rarely do we focus on our most favourite parts. It is well documented that being positive and optimistic actually supports good health. When we are healthy, we feel great. When we feel great, we exude self-confidence. All these positive feelings bubble up and we reap the rewards tenfold. We look better, we have more energy and our wellness definitely improves.

It is time to be forgiving, accepting and loving towards your body and it is time to accentuate all your beautiful qualities and attributes. Everyone is uniquely beautiful, so enhance all of your favourite bits and be sure to share with the world what makes you special.

The following is a wonderful exercise to remind yourself of all your positive qualities and attributes and it is something I have done many a time with clients. I call it the 'I love me' exercise.

'I LOVE ME' EXERCISE:

To begin, take a blank piece of paper.

Grab a pen or a marker and draw yourself on this piece of paper.

Draw an outline of your whole body, your face, your hair.

Draw it as accurately as you can.

Once you have done that, I want you to identify all the things that are beautiful about you.

Really acknowledge all the things you love. Look at yourself as a whole being, focussing on everything that makes up you.

Then write each beautiful quality down on the page surrounding your image.

Don't be afraid to do this exercise. It is healthy to remind yourself of your gorgeousness just in case it has slipped your mind.

For example, you may write around your image —

- I love my beautiful eyes.

- I love my long, graceful neck.

- I love my strength.

- I have beautiful skin on my décolletage.

- I love my shapely hips.

- I have a kind and loving heart.

- I love my ability to be generous.

- I love how I am so funny.

- I love my gorgeous wavy hair.

- I love my curvy tummy.

Nothing is off limits here. Each sentence must start with 'I love my' and you must acknowledge at least five of your amazing qualities and attributes. You can include, body, mind and spirit attributes. Once you have done this, place this drawing in a spot where you will regularly see it; maybe on the bathroom mirror or maybe even in your underwear drawer if you want to keep it private. Just make sure you look at it at least once a day. Once you start to recognise all of your beauty, as it penetrates your soul, it will become easier to accept that you are actually beautiful. Loving yourself is the key to making peace with yourself.

STEP FOUR: BODY, MIND, SPIRIT NOURISHMENT

When it comes to achieving inner peace, we absolutely must consider the big picture. Wellness and balance encompass the body, the mind and the spirit. These three areas are all connected and we need to accept the fact that each day it is vital to nourish all three. Delegating time to each area and understanding that we must keep a positive flow of energy happening continuously for our systems to feel balanced is vital.

The body, mind and spirit work as a system of energy. The energy flow in each area can be fluid and positive or it can be stagnant, depending on our actual state of being. From moment to moment our state of being can change, depending on what is happening around us. It can also change depending on how we are treating these systems. Unhealthy food versus healthy food, positive thoughts versus negative thoughts, movement and sunlight versus doing nothing and darkness. Ideally we want the body, mind and spirit to be balanced and energised on all levels. The goal is to be in alignment in all areas so that we experience wellness and the key to achieving this is to nourish our system as a whole.

When our body, mind and spirit is balanced, we feel a sense of peace and contentment. We naturally treat ourselves and especially our body with love and respect. We have a sense of purpose and we automatically feel motivated and optimistic every day. We feel energised and calm but when our body, mind and spirit are out of alignment, we experience the exact opposite. In order to make peace with our bodies as well as ourselves, ideally your goal should be to harmonise each area so that wellness, self-confidence and self-acceptance is effortless. Let's simplify the basic ingredients required in each system to achieve balance. Breaking it down this way will show you that it is much easier than you think.

The Body:

- A clean, beautiful healthy diet.

- A wide variety of fresh, wholesome, nutritious foods

- Exercise

- Rest

- Sleep

- Focussed breathing

- Water

- Sunlight

- Love

The Mind:

- Positive thoughts

- Stimulation

- Rest

- Sleep

- Focussed breathing

- Meditation

- Sunshine

- Love

The Spirit:

- Self-love

- Peace

- Prayer, affirmations or meditation

- A balanced body and mind.

All of the above practices support good health and wellness. Maintaining your mind and spirit in a state of peace will automatically support wellbeing as well as a healthy body if you are eating correctly.

You don't have to become a yogi or a spiritual guru to reap the benefits of practising meditation, affirmations or any other spiritual practice. Taking five minutes each morning to focus on your breathing is hugely beneficial in itself. Focussing on your breathing is something you can do throughout the day, anytime, anywhere. When you are feeling stressed or overwhelmed, just take a moment to stop and breathe.

It may seem a little strange, but one of the best things you can do in times of high stress or anxiety is actually, not much at all. What I mean by this is just to be quiet, still and observant of your breath. Breath is the foundation of all life. It is the connection between body, mind and spirit. Through breath control, we can manage our stress, calm ourselves and gain clearness of mind. It can even boost your mood and affect how you see yourself and the world. If you only remember this following piece of information when you are feeling overwhelmed, whether you are beating up on yourself or just feeling stressed and exhausted, and that is to just take three deep, slow breaths. Taking three deep, long slow breaths will help calm the mind, body and spirit. It will instantly bring everything back into balance. It is instant nourishment. Breathing is something we all do and something which we rarely pay much attention to. Focussing on breathing is one of the most powerful ways to calm and connect the body, mind and spirit, and it is an essential tool for wellness and balance. In the quest to make peace with your body, focussing on breathing is a perfect place to begin.

If you need to make peace with your body, it is important to really accept the fact that you must support and nourish your mind and spirit as well. Your goal is to attain complete peace and let me remind you that you are made up of so much more than just muscle and skin.

STEP FIVE: EATING FOR A PEACEFUL SYSTEM

When your diet is out of control and it is time to make changes, the first step on this journey is to consult a health care practitioner. Ensure that you have a complete medical checkup that includes a blood test to check your sugar levels and cholesterol levels, as well as a full blood analysis. Always seek medical advice and be responsible for your own health and well-being. Knowing what your body is doing on the inside is the first step in promoting a peaceful system.

Now I have tried most diets, and as I have said, I may have seen some results initially, but nothing long term. When I trained in nutrition, I was taught to separate real food from artificial food. If it came in a box, had a label, was loaded with ingredients that I couldn't understand it was moved to the artificial food list. If it was highly processed, it was also moved over. I was trained to avoid the artificial food list at all costs, as this list of foods promoted inflammation of the system. Inflammation of the system led to premature ageing, disease, obesity, internal aggravation and fatigue. It also led to complete discontentment of the body as bloating was often a result of these foods. Think snack foods, cured meats, white bread, white pasta, cakes, biscuits, sweets, high-fat take-away foods, pizza, burgers, hot chips, soft drinks, diet drinks, sauces, pretty much anything that had some form of human interference became the enemy. Now, if you have just had a little freak out and thought, *Oh God, there is nothing else to eat when that is all off limits, then it is definitely time to retrain the brain as well as rethink your food choices.*

Good nutrition really is the basis of good health and wellness. We really must consume beautiful healthy wholesome fresh foods daily if we want to achieve wellness. For your body to function properly, you need to clean it up and re-train your brain to eat real food. Real food is whole, unprocessed and unrefined. It is pasture-raised, grass fed and wild. It is local, seasonal and organic. It is found in the ground and of course on trees.

Eat more fresh fruit, fresh vegetables, lean protein, fresh fish, dairy, grains, fresh herbs, and fresh spices. Think colour, raw, fresh, and simple. Now let me make this clear, everyone is different and there are certain fresh foods that disagree with me from time to time, but on the whole, fresh, healthy wholesome food supports a healthy body. If you really have a super-sensitive system, it can be a process of elimination to find the right balance. There are some amazing dieticians and nutritionists around that will work with you to find that right balance if you do not know where to start and the beauty of this is that they treat your individual requirements.

It's all about balance, moderation and committing daily to making these positive healthy choices for your body. So where do you start if you need to quit dieting and embrace healthy eating as a lifestyle?

1: Commit to only shopping the perimeter of your supermarket for groceries. This area contains all the beautiful, fresh produce. All the pre-packaged and processed foods are located in the central aisles.

2: Eat fruit and vegetables raw as often as possible – choose salads over cooking.

3: Eat a rainbow every day. When it comes to fresh, wholesome food, every coloured fruit and vegetable contains unique phytonutrients and minerals that will assist with anti-ageing, wellness and energy.

4: Eat protein and carbohydrates at every meal. Aim for balance to keep your blood sugar stable.

5: Don't underestimate the power of fresh food as a way to heal your body. Food is medicine.

6: Fresh herbs and spices also have healing properties. Use them abundantly.

7: Variety is the spice of life, so don't eat the same foods over and over again. Shake it up and be adventurous.

8: Train your brain to recognise that anything with a food label or is contained in a box could cause an upset system. Be observant and educate yourself on food labels and ingredients. This way you can choose wisely.

9: Drink plenty of water. Water is involved in so many processes in the body. Being just 2% dehydrated can start to hinder your body's ability to perform at its best.

10: Quit dieting and embrace healthy nutrition. Make healthy choices a lifestyle and a habit.

A diet is all about focussing on the calories you eat and the calories you burn. Dieting is about restrictions. Eating fresh, healthy wholesome food and keeping it balanced and real will promote a peaceful system. Success is then defined in terms of how these healthy changes make you feel about yourself and your body and not about the number on the scales.

STEP SIX: MOVE IT

Just as I have experimented with diets, I have experimented with exercise. I have joined gyms, done aerobics, Pilates,
weights, yoga, dance classes, boxing, laps in an Olympic pool,
running and tried all the exercise equipment that promised
thin thighs and perfect abs all while you sit relaxed enjoying
a latte!

I have torn ligaments, tendons, ended up on crutches and
even hurt my back. I have experienced the whole no pain/
no gain scenario, and quite frankly, it doesn't suit me. When
I commit to an exercise program, I go full steam ahead.
The battery is fully charged and then I challenge myself
continuously until I flatline. Now, I know plenty of exercise
experts who would say, that's great, but I beg to differ. It may
be a great way to exercise if you can keep this routine up and
in perspective, but if you are an all-or-nothing kind of girl like
myself, it can be a problem. At some point when it all gets too
hard and I have sustained an injury, I quit.

A couple of years ago, I had committed to climbing our
local hiking track daily. Steep and high and reasonably
challenging, it would take approximately twenty to thirty
minutes to complete, depending on your level of fitness. It
is hard work but when you get to the top, the views of the
natural environment are breathtaking. This walk is a real
push for me and yet, for others, it is a walk in the park. One
particular day, as I was dragging myself to the top, gasping
for air and reminding myself that the burn would be worth it,

I encountered a very young man who was walking the same track. He too was struggling, puffing and sweating as well. He stopped about a metre in front of me, turned and said, "This is tough isn't it?" I said "Definitely!" I asked him how long he had been doing the walk for and he told me he had only just started back that week. He then said to me, "I use to be really fit, but then I got sick. I had leukaemia and I nearly didn't survive. My sister gave me a bone marrow transplant and now I am in remission. This week, I decided to reclaim my fitness and here I am. Every day I am grateful because, well, I am alive!" I was overwhelmed by his humility, his fighting spirit and his absolute appreciation for every breath he was taking on this climb. I congratulated him and told him how inspiring he was and how glad I was to have met him.

As I continued up the climb, an elderly gentleman came jogging down the track. He was fighting fit. He looked at me and smiled and said, "You are almost there." I said to him, "Wow! You are making me feel guilty and really unfit." He laughed and said, "I have been running this track every day for twenty-seven years religiously. I started working on my fitness when I turned fifty as I had a scare with my health and I knew I had to make changes. Twenty-seven years later I am still running this track every day!" That made him seventy-seven. Then he said to me, "It's never too late to start something new. You just have to believe that you can do it and you have to find an exercise that you want to do. You have to look forward to it. That is the secret!" And with that, he kept running.

That conversation made me realise that I had always looked

at exercise as a chore and I hadn't actually considered that perhaps there were gentler ways to move and get fit. It's a given. We need to exercise the body, but there are so many ways to move. I had only ever considered the traditional forms which, quite frankly, I didn't really enjoy.

It's a good idea to define your goals and look at your history with exercise. I didn't really enjoy exercise. Doing something I didn't enjoy to begin my day or end my day really wasn't uplifting. I acknowledged also that I needed to find some way of exercising that I would actually look forward too. I had to schedule in at least thirty minutes a day with some joyous, energising activity, not just for a month but for life.

There are just millions of ways to get the blood pumping. The goal is to find a workout that you will willingly do consistently. I am not one for hardcore boot camp, so once again for me I have had to retrain the brain to accept that really, anything that gets your heart rate up is considered to be exercise. I have had far too many injuries over the years as well, so I tend to lean towards the side of caution now with a gentler approach so that I don't put myself out of action completely. I do know a lot of people who disagree and despite their many injuries they push past them, but that technique just doesn't work for me.

I decided to look back to what it was I did as a child that I absolutely loved when it came to exercise. I spent most of my days swimming in our pool or at the beach; I would just swim for hours pretending that I was a mermaid. At the beach, we would body surf all afternoon and that was so invigorating.

We would walk for hours along the beach, feet in the water, sand between our toes; it was healing. We would put on our favourite records and dance for hours in the lounge room. We would roller skate on weekends. We would go round and round that skate rink listening to the tunes of Abba and the Bay City Rollers. If you are finding that it is difficult to find an exercise regime that excites, then often the key is casting your mind back to what really made you feel happy, invigorated and excited as a kid. If that isn't the answer either, then how about considering just consciously moving more as a part of your daily lifestyle. Can you incorporate short ten minute mini workouts throughout the day? Breaking it up can be hugely beneficial. Can you do a ten minute walk as soon as you wake up? Can you park further away and walk to work? Can you get up from your desk and walk down to the receptionist rather than calling her? Can you pop outside at lunch time and spend five minutes in the fresh air breathing and stretching? Can you do a ten minute bike ride or swim after work? Can you attend a dance class, a Zumba class or a salsa class once a week? Can you take the stairs religiously instead of the lift? Can you increase your walking pace when you are running errands? Can you do squats and lunges while showering? There are a million opportunities presented to you over the day where you can just move more and even incorporate effective specific exercises without it taking up too much time. Picking up the pace physically is a brilliant place to begin to increase fitness levels.

Top Tips:

1: Consult your health care practitioner before starting a new exercise regime.

2: Write a plan of action.

3: Find some form of activity that moves your body and your soul.

4: Be consistent. Habits are formed by repeatedly practising a behaviour and you need to make exercise a daily habit.

5: Keep it simple. When we overcomplicate things and make it too difficult to begin with, we are more inclined to quit.

6: If you need someone to motivate you, find a partner to share the journey with. This creates accountability.

7: Move more at every opportunity.

8: Accept that your body needs movement regularly to thrive and be healthy.

9: Stretch.

10: It is never too late to start.

We all know that the benefits of exercise are enormous both physically and mentally and your body will respond to it with more energy. The key is to find the type of exercise that not only improves your health and wellbeing, but it also lifts you up and makes you feel good about yourself. No matter what type of exercise inspires you, whether it is boot camp, training, running, swimming, dancing, riding, walking, salsa dancing, or skipping, remember our bodies thrive when we move more.

STEP SEVEN: THE SECRET

Throughout history and even today, women will search out ways to look younger, slimmer and more beautiful. Quick fix pills, treatments and elixirs promising youthfulness, weight loss and anti-ageing are plentiful. I believe as women, we have every right to do whatever we want when it comes to making ourselves feel more confident. I personally love beauty products, hair care, make up and I love fashion. I delight in all things that promote feeling good and I really enjoy experimenting with different products. It is important though to remember that beauty and confidence extends far beyond your face, it starts from within and encompasses many things – energy, personality, life force, good health. It's a combination of many different aspects that make you uniquely beautiful. That being said, we can all make a difference to how we feel and we can improve our energy levels, which in turn will make us glow and radiate confidence. This will certainly help with self-esteem and will promote that feeling of vitality.

Anti-ageing, good health, beauty, confidence, energy all start internally. If you are spending hundreds of dollars on beauty treatments, beauty products and vitamins and you are not supporting the body with good nutrition and healthy habits, you are literally throwing your money away. By changing the foods you eat from unhealthy to healthy, you can radically change your appearance and how you feel. Think about that when planning your meals.

Top Tips to promote internal peace:

1: Eating foods raw is the key to obtaining the most beautifying vitamins, enzymes and nutrition. You do not need to become a raw food advocate by any means, but just consider the opportunities you have at meal times to eat raw food. Eat more salads and fresh fruit, a piece of fruit with breakfast, a salad and piece of fruit at lunch, there's a good start. Any type of heat will destroy some of the nutrients but lightly steamed will retain some, so consider steaming vegetables at dinner with fish, followed by another piece of fruit. How easy is that, and such a positive step towards making internal peace.

2: One thing that depletes energy and wellbeing is bad digestion. Take a good quality probiotic every single day, as probiotics promote a healthy digestive environment and play a critical role in immune function. A healthy digestive system equates to more energy.

3: Take a tablespoon of raw unfiltered apple cider vinegar before meals. This also helps to promote healthy digestion and will work on cleansing the bowel as well as the digestive tract.

4: Quit diet drinks permanently. We have all so willingly convinced ourselves into believing that it is actually 'diet' and that we are consuming far less calories than normal soft drinks. Our systems really go into shock when we consume diet drinks. The enormous amounts of caffeine contained in many diet drinks can act as a diuretic and the high levels of phosphorous contained can also drain the calcium from your body. Diet drinks and soft drinks of any kind will rob your body of precious minerals that are important to maintaining a well-balanced system.

5: A lot of people think that by not eating, you will be rewarded with weight loss, but this is not true. If you decrease your food intake dramatically, your body will assume there is a food shortage and it will try to conserve energy. This means minimal weight loss and your body will naturally hold onto whatever fat your body is carrying to protect itself. If your goal is to lose weight, eat regular fresh, clean meals throughout the course of the day.

6: Keeping a food diary is an excellent first step in assessing how you eat and why you eat the way you do, as well as recording your eating habits. It will help you target your current eating problems and assist you in addressing reasons why things may be out of control. Keeping a food diary will give you a firsthand look at the types and amounts of food that you are eating. For example, you will be able to see the amounts of fruits and vegetables you are consuming daily; probably not nearly enough! Keeping a food diary can also help you better understand eating behavioural patterns. You will be able to see when and if stressful situations trigger emotional eating. It will help you to be accountable for your food choices and with working out food allergies and intolerances. It can also assist people who need to gain weight to recognise how little calories they are consuming or to help them stay on track with regular eating.

7: Aspartame, Saccharin, BAH and BUT, Mono-sodium glutamate, Potassium bromate, Sodium nitrate and nitrate – these are some of the worst artificial ingredient offenders. Artificial sweeteners and other artificial ingredients that preserve, thicken or conceal are artificial, which pretty much means that they are not supposed to go into your body. It is time to look at what you are consuming and take responsibility.

8: Make a concerted effort to drink water throughout the day. This will help the kidneys to process and eliminate any unwanted toxins and keep you energised.

9: Skin brushing on a daily basis can help with the flow of lymph around the body and therefore will assist with the removal of toxins.

10: Not getting enough sleep can lead to cravings for sugary foods. This throws your body into a spike and crash cycle. When you give in and have a sugary treat, the sugar creates an insulin rush. Instantly you feel better but shortly afterwards, you will crash and burn. Ensure you aim to get a good night's sleep.

11: Drink a glass of water at the onset of a sugar craving.

12: Don't confuse hunger with thirst. Sometimes our body is signalling us for water.

13: One tablespoon of flaxseed oil in the morning will help to control cravings.

14: After about 45 minutes of being sedentary, our cells start to burn less energy. This process actually slows down your metabolism making it a lot harder to keep your weight in a healthy range. Set an alarm or a reminder and make the effort to move every hour after you have been sitting for a while. It only takes 30 seconds of movement to reactivate your cells.

15: Apples are jam packed with nutrients, so it makes sense to eat more fruit and vegetables. You will get a ton of vitamins straight up without the expense of the vitamin pills.

16: The occasional glass of red wine or the odd beer is enjoyable and there are certainly some health benefits when having the odd drink, but things decline beyond those moderate levels with wine, beer, and other alcoholic beverages. High consumption of alcohol provokes chronic inflammation, especially of the liver and oesophagus and causes open pores and dull lifeless skin. Alcohol equals lots of empty calories.

17: Learn to be mindful. Allow your stomach and brain receptors the privilege of catching up with each other before you decide that you need more food. Chances are you are already full.

18: Herbs and spices certainly can provide protective properties and they can reduce inflammation. Inflammation has been identified as a precursor to many chronic diseases and conditions and herbs and spices can assist in healing the body. My personal favourite is turmeric powder. Researchers are looking into the role of turmeric in brain health and protection against cognitive decline associated with ageing.

19: Fibre plays a very important role in nutrition and is very beneficial in many aspects of health and wellness. It can assist in healthy weight management and it is also important to maintain a high level of fibre to keep the digestive and cardiovascular system healthy.

20: If you have a bad day and eat a whole lot of unhealthy food, don't beat yourself up. Get back to healthy eating at the very next meal. Don't allow one bad setback to stop you from achieving good health and wellness. We are all human, move forward.

It is definitely a combination of many things that lead to health, wellbeing, and internal peace. Solely focussing on eating one food isn't going to help you achieve optimum results. It is daily commitment and taking a holistic approach to your body, mind and spirit that will boost your overall health and wellbeing and create balance.

So what is the secret to internal peace? We must aim to reduce internal inflammation. Unhealthy eating, too much alcohol, too much sugar, too much stress, are all contributing causes of internal inflammation. Internal inflammation is the precursor to disease, premature ageing and an unhealthy body as well as a foggy mind. Reduce this internal inflammation and you will instantly make peace with your body. The above twenty tips will move you forward towards regaining a healthy system.

Be sure to incorporate every aspect of support for your mind, body and soul. Meditation, rest, physical exercise, healthy wholesome food at every opportunity – these are all vital elements to promoting wellness and reducing internal inflammation.

STEP EIGHT: FILL UP YOUR SELF ESTEEM BOWL

If you feel like your self-esteem is at its lowest, it is important to top up that tank. Do not let anyone undermine your self-confidence. Ignore media trends, criticism from others and stop with the self-criticism. Start using phrases like I am, I will, I can, in regards to yourself. Commit to thinking about all that you can do to feel amazing and all that you can achieve with the power of positive thinking.

Top tips to fill up that bowl:

1: Visualise in your mind's eye how you will look and feel when you have finally made peace with your body. Visualise the activities you will do when you have more energy. Visualisation is a great tool to help you achieve your goals so every night when you retire, visualise the new, healthier you.

2: Remind yourself daily that you can absolutely achieve all of your dreams and goals.

3: Completely believe in yourself. Back every decision you make especially in regards to making peace with your body.

4:    Before you go to sleep, see the energetic you jumping out of bed in the morning ready to take on a healthy lifestyle.

5:    Affirm the following statement daily, *I am whole and well. I am releasing imbalance from every cell in my body. I am reclaiming my health and wellness. I am listening to my body. I am healthy and vibrant. I am happy.* Your mind is paying attention, so talk lovingly to yourself.

6:    Remind yourself constantly –
That you are worthwhile.
That you are good enough.
That you are in control.
That you are beautiful.

7:    Don't rely on someone else to lift you up. Do it for yourself.

8:    Set realistic expectations for yourself.

9:    Perfection is simply unattainable for any of us so quite simply, let it go.

10:    You may have been at war for a while with yourself. As you begin your journey towards wellness and self-love, make sure you take something valuable away from the battle. Unhealthy habits and the negative effects they have are an opportunity for learning and growth. Self-pity is a fairly natural thing. Although it's good to question things and reflect on challenging circumstances, actually wallowing and really immersing yourself in self-pity is extremely unhealthy.

Practice self-esteem fostering thoughts and behaviour every day and believe that anything is possible. Take personal responsibility for your life and consciously choose to start working towards optimum wellness. Choose to focus on what is right about you and not what is wrong and find the strength to take gigantic, wonderful, positive steps forward with or without the fairy-tale ending. Your thoughts create your world. Don't waste your precious energy on negative ones. Appreciate your body, your mind, your spirit, your life.

STEP NINE: HIGH-FIVE YOURSELF

I have had so many amazing experiences in my life to date, I tend to forget some days to acknowledge the amazing things I have done. It really is important to stop and take stock of all those ground-breaking changes, breakthroughs and achievements often.

I personally prefer to acknowledge things privately. When I look back over the years, I have had the great privilege of working with some iconic people. I have had the opportunity to take my experiences and help raise money for charities associated with cystic fibrosis, cerebral palsy, breast cancer and cancer. My husband and I also had the great fortune of assisting an amazing nun for some years who worked as a missionary in Papua New Guinea. She lived in a dangerous area and selflessly devoted her life to teaching children who were denied an education. We contributed by supplying books and educational materials to these beautiful children for some years. We would take care of this incredible woman every three months for two weeks when she would make her way back to Australia to recharge her weary soul. She did this well into her eighties and passed away just recently. We couldn't go with her, but we could do something worthwhile to assist her. It was only recently when I was scrolling through social media and saw a post by a girl who was about to head to Indonesia to do some volunteer work, that I was reminded of what significant contributions I had made over the years. When I stopped and really started to look back, I felt real satisfaction that I had made a contribution to these incredible charities. Then as quick as a wink, I moved on to what I could do next … but that's just how I roll!

We often get so caught up with everyday life that we do not take the time to acknowledge our personal achievements or even our contributions to the world. It's important to do it as this is another powerful way to top up that self-esteem tank. There are many who need to continuously post their achievements on Facebook. Checking the number of likes and 'Wahoo' comments just fuels their satisfaction. Each to their own, but if for some crazy reason Facebook was to shut down, can they still achieve that same sense of fulfilment without the constant accolades?

There is a massive difference between shouting your success

to the world, and actually stopping and really giving yourself permission to feel a sense of pride, satisfaction and achievement. To know you have made a difference or achieved a goal, no matter how big or small, is a sure-fire way to promote happiness, positivity and to motivate you to make even more changes.

I know it sounds a little crazy, but even when I am out to dinner now and I order a healthy meal over an unhealthy meal, I silently congratulate myself. Last year, I fell down a flight of stairs and sustained a few really painful injuries; one twisted ankle, nerve damage to both shins, a fractured wrist, a cracked cheek, an injury to my hip, back and neck as well as a big bump and cut to the back of my head. It seemed to take forever to be able to get back out and exercise. My whole body was out of alignment. My husband would take me down to the Esplanade walking track in the afternoons when I was recovering. I couldn't walk far and I would make it to a certain point, collapse in tears and pain and he would say, "I will go get the car". I would pull myself together and say, "No, I can make it back". Day by day, I was able to walk a bit further and day by day it was a bit easier.

It really took me a whole year to recover from all the twists, pulls and bruising sustained, but I am walking every day now for an hour easily and can even climb our apartment stairs, all twelve floors with ease. Every time I do this, I really feel a sense of achievement; it feels so good to move forward. It was hard work, but I really do acknowledge each walk, climb and activity that I do now, especially when I don't experience pain. I really high-five myself every single step of the way.

Top Tips:

1:   Look back and really acknowledge all of your high-five moments.

2:   Start focussing on all of your achievements daily.

3:   Acknowledge your failures. Learn from them, let them go and then move on.

4:   Self acknowledgement gives you the power to realise that you have the ability to achieve anything you really set your mind and heart on.

5:   Acknowledge big achievements but acknowledge those small ones just as vigorously.

6:   Give yourself permission to celebrate your own success. Don't rely on other people to acknowledge your achievements. Do it yourself.

7:   Surround yourself with your achievements so you can see them daily. For example, photos are a great reminder of your success.

8:   Write down your achievements daily. You will be amazed at what you have accomplished over a twenty-four hour period when you write it down and then look back at it all.

9: Celebrate in your own way. You may just take some time out to relax, you may reward yourself with something special, or you may simply revel quietly in the moment privately. Whatever it is that brings you that feeling of achievement, be sure to immerse yourself in it.

10: When you stop to acknowledge your achievements daily, you create the energy needed to fuel more goals.

Every positive step forward is worth celebrating. It doesn't matter how big or how small. Having the ability to be your own personal cheer squad is another glorious way to build up your self- esteem. So three cheers to you!

STEP TEN: IT IS NEVER TOO LATE TO MAKE PEACE

I know women who are still battling with their bodies in their seventies. I have worked with women at this age that are still dieting and criticising themselves day in and day out. It is exhausting. If you have struggled in any way, shape or form with weight issues, whether they be overweight or under-weight. If you have struggled with low self-esteem or have spent days criticising your appearance or your abilities, well you know just how depleting it is.

Life is way too short to continuously wage war with yourself every day. I can assure you, it is never too late to begin again and make a new start and create brand new healthy habits. At any age, we can make the decision to change the future course of our health, our life and how we live. It is a conscious choice to make that change, to commit to the changes and then really feel the difference that accompanies self-love. It may be that you have to take baby steps every day to begin, but these steps are still moving you forward. You may take giant steps forward daily once you have made the decision to make peace. Whatever you choose, don't look back. If you have been at war with yourself for far too many years, it is time to make peace. The changes you make right now will ultimately lead you to freedom.

Top Tips to make peace now:

1:    Make the decision to stop the war.

2:    Commit to creating new habits.

3:    Quit negative self-talk immediately.

4:    Acknowledge your beauty, your beautiful qualities and your uniqueness.

5:    Quit dieting now.

6:    Embrace healthy eating as a lifestyle and work towards finding what foods support *your* body.

7:    Accentuate your positives.

8: Start to acknowledge and celebrate every step you take forward.

9: No more procrastination, complaining or excuses.

10: Take responsibility for your wellness. Do it now.

You have one life to live. Don't waste days feeling inferior based on weight, size, appearance or lack of self-worth. Quit punishing yourself. If you need help to take the first step towards making peace with your body and your inner critic, be brave enough to seek assistance. Nowadays, we have an abundance of health care practitioners, councillors, coaches and trainers that can take you by the hand and lead you forward. Remember, ultimately you have to be the one to do the work and make the choices. No-one can do that part for you.

Make the changes that will lift you up and allow you to shine. Your life is precious and so are you. You deserve to feel beautiful. You deserve to celebrate every inch of you. You deserve to feel peace. The greatest gift you can give to yourself and to those people in your life that you cherish is self-love. Invest in your wellness. You are priceless and in case you have forgotten, let me remind you that you are beautiful. You are unique and there is no-one else on this planet like you.

As women, we must band together and celebrate our ability to change the world.

We must commit to recognising each other's intelligence and integrity based on our hearts and our minds.

Let us commit to lifting each other up.

My wish for you is peace.

—Jo Ettles

WRITE YOUR BODY A LETTER

Wave the white flag and make peace with your body

Dear Body

_____

_____

_____

_____

_____

_____

_____

_____

_____

_____

_____

_____

_____

_____

_____

_____

With love

MY LIFESTYLE PLAN

Your lifestyle plan is a valuable tool and a wonderful first step
in turning your world around.
You deserve to nourish and nurture yourself every day.
Schedule in ME TIME and HEALTHY HABITS to remind you
that your wellness is a priority.

_____

_____

_____

_____

_____

_____

_____

_____

_____

_____

_____

_____

'I LOVE ME' EXERCISE

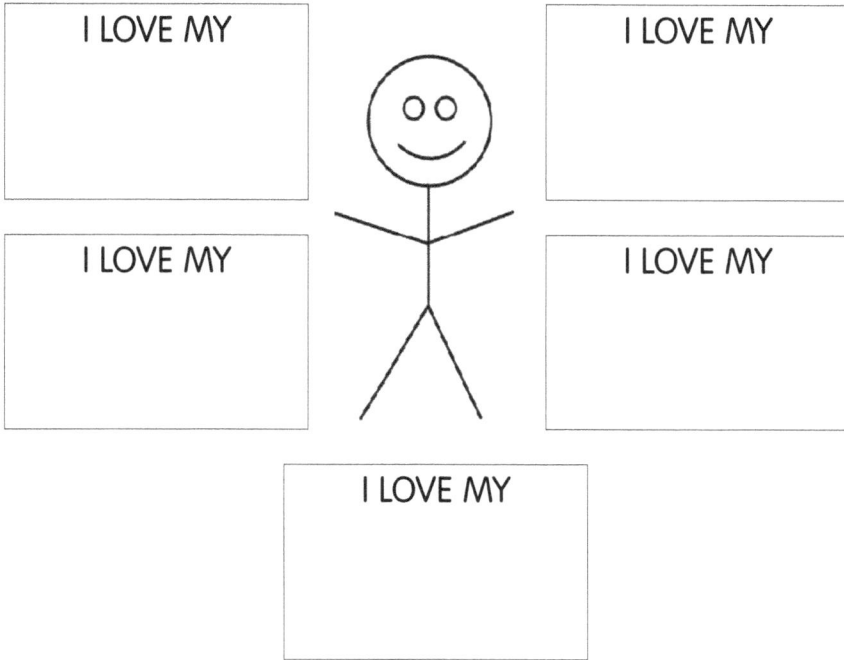

I LOVE MY	I LOVE MY

I LOVE MY	I LOVE MY

I LOVE MY

Really acknowledge all the things you love about YOU.

Acknowledge every one of your beautiful qualities and features
and write it down.
It is healthy to remind yourself of your gorgeousness!
Be creative with your stick figure. She needs some love
and attention ❤

MY AFFIRMATIONS

Create your own affirmations and plant positive seeds daily
into your mind.

Begin your affirmations with

I can — I will — I am

Fill your mind with what is right about you and
not what is wrong.

I am whole

I am healthy

I am good enough

I am beautiful

I completely love and accept myself

_____

_____

_____

_____

_____

_____

_____

_____

_____

_____

_____

EXAMPLE—FOOD DIARY

	Monday	Tuesday	Wednesday	Thursday	Friday	Saturday	Sunday
Breakfast							
Lunch							
Dinner							
Snacks							
Exercise & Water intake							

www.ingramcontent.com/pod-product-compliance
Lightning Source LLC
Chambersburg PA
CBHW020245290326
41930CB00038B/402